Why Can't I Have Faith?

Why Can't I Have Faith?

Working out belief in the Post-Modern World

FRANCIS BRIDGER

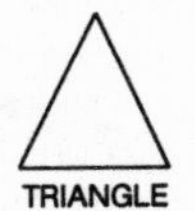

First published in Great Britain 1998
Triangle Books
Holy Trinity Church
Marylebone Road
London NW1 4DU

British Library Cataloguing-in-Publication Data

A catalogue record of this book is available from the British Library

ISBN 0-281-05006-6

Typeset by Pioneer Associates, Perthshire
Printed in Great Britain by
Caledonian International Glasgow

Contents

To the people of St Mark's
from whom
I have learned so much

Introduction

A few years ago I ran a discussion group by the name of *Agnostics Anonymous*. Its purpose was to identify and discuss subjects the group felt to be obstacles to Christian belief. The relationship between science and faith, the problem of suffering and the person of Jesus Christ quickly emerged as the key issues.

This book is a direct outcome of those discussions. What I have tried to do, therefore, is to take agnosticism seriously by dividing the book into three parts, each one of which is devoted to one of the topics above. In turn each part breaks down into three chapters. The first argues a strong agnostic case; the second a more moderate one; and the third a Christian response to both. This pattern structures all three parts of the book so that the reader (I hope) will feel I have been fair to the range of agnostic views which are commonly held on the subjects under discussion.

But, as I argue in the concluding chapter, the enormity of the issues does not allow us perpetually to sit on the fence. Agnosticism that *refuses* to make up its mind will always be unsatisfactory. If nothing else, the character and claims of Jesus Christ force us to choose.

It is my hope, then, that Christians will find this a helpful book to give to their agnostic friends and that the latter will find it stimulating. If either of these objectives is realized, the labour will have been worth it.

Finally, I should like to thank those who have enabled me to complete *Why Can't I Have Faith?* in the midst of busy parish life; Rachel Boulding for her editorial patience and tactful suggestions; the scientist whose name is unknown to me but who checked Chapters 1 to 3 and whose comments I found invaluable; and Andy Norman, my agnostic friend who not only contributed to the group discussions but also later taught me how to use the computer on which this book was produced. I am grateful to them all.

Francis Bridger

PART ONE
Science and Faith

1
The Triumph of Science

I for one must be content to remain an Agnostic.
Charles Darwin

Ask a group of people whether they think that science has been successful and you will probably get a blank stare or a knowing smile, depending on whether they regard you as stupid or just plain mad. Such has been the phenomenal advance of science over the last three centuries that only an ignoramus or a fool would dream of questioning its success. At least, this would be the general view. In this chapter we are going to see how the situation looks from the standpoint of an agnostic who assumes that science has made religious faith obsolete.

The case for the triumph of science over faith begins not with high-flown philosophy but with the practicalities of life. No impartial observer could seriously doubt that without science we would be in a dire state: no electricity, no power of any kind (other than fire perhaps, but even the application of that employs some rudimentary scientific principles), hardly any medicine beyond leeches and magic potions, no life-saving technology and certainly no mechanized transport. For most of us it is impossible to imagine.

And the list does not end there. From the mundane shopping trip to the luxury holiday abroad, we are surrounded by gadgets and devices made possible only by the application of science. Indeed, only to think back ten or fifteen years is to remember when word processors were almost unknown and computers confined to the realms of high-tech scientific research. This book would have been laboriously written by hand or typed on a simple typewriter. Put simply, science has been the engine of unbelievable human progress.

But the triumph of science lies not only in its practical achievements – which is all that most of us are concerned with most of the time – but also in its method. This is nothing short of revolutionary. In science we have a method so powerful in its results that it has swept all before it. Indeed, the real triumph of science has not been to provide us with more and more material progress or even more ways of relieving human suffering (important though these are). Rather, its victory has been in enabling us to understand how the world works, down to the smallest atom and beyond, and how we can shape it for our own ends. No longer need we be subject to the arbitrary whims and capricious forces of nature. Even these are within our grasp.

Just as importantly (and this lies at the heart of the agnostic case), science offers us a way of understanding the nature of reality without having to invoke God, divine agency or the supernatural. By means of the scientific method we are able develop theories to cover every area of life from the internal workings of the human mind to the origins of the universe. Indeed, it is now possible to speak of constructing what has become known only half-jokingly as a Theory of Everything, and in more technical language a Grand Unified Theory. In Stephen Hawking's memorable words,

> If we do discover a complete theory . . . then we shall all . . . be able to take part in the discussion of why it is that we and the universe exist. If we find the answer to that, it would be the ultimate triumph of human reason – for then we would truly know the mind of God.

Whereas our forebears sought to plug the holes in their knowledge of the universe by invoking God (the so-called 'God of the gaps'), modern science deliberately discards such a tactic. For the holes are there to be plugged, not by taking refuge in supernatural mysteries and religious gobbledegook but by the operation of the human mind. We do not require God to fill in the missing bits because as science continues its triumphal progress we shall eventually find there are no bits left. Until we possess such knowledge, of course, we must remain content to say that we don't have all the answers yet. We have begun the journey but have not reached its end. As science continues to reach further and further, the mysteries will become fewer and fewer. This is quite a different thing from assigning unanswered questions to the realm of supernatural agency.

What is more, history is on the agnostic's side. Religious interpretations of physical events are everywhere in retreat, and have been for three centuries. What were once 'miracles' are now everyday occurrences, as our hospitals and medical centres testify. What were hitherto seen as supernatural phenomena – such as demons and evil spirits – can now be explained in wholly natural terms. Where devils used to prowl unseen, we now recognize the effects of a traumatized psyche. (Thanks be to Freud!)

As the last verse of Matthew Arnold's poem 'Dover Beach' puts it:

> The Sea of Faith
> Was once, too, at the full, and round earth's shore
> Lay like the folds of a bright girdle furl'd.
> But now I only hear
> Its melancholy, long, withdrawing roar,
> Retreating, to the breath
> Of the night-wind, down the vast edges drear
> And naked shingles of the world.

This then is the gist of the argument behind the case for agnosticism. To all intents and purposes, science has rendered the claims of religion obsolete. All that now remains is to flesh out the argument.

1. The Appliance of Science

The phenomenal success of science over the past three centuries can be seen on every side. We can point to revolutions in farming, medicine, work and leisure which have fuelled economic and social progress throughout the world. Similarly, the scientific method applied to human societies through the so-called 'human sciences' has enabled us to understand more about how they function and to plan social and economic polices more effectively. Medicine alone has saved the lives of countless millions who would otherwise have perished, and has brought about a vast increase in the length of life for others. The problem is that we in the West are so used to this that we easily forget how revolutionary the contribution of science has been.

In seventeenth-century England, for example, the average life expectancy of boys born to even the richest families was no more than thirty years. A third of them died before the age of five. Today they could expect to live to seventy or beyond. Meanwhile, for those who did survive, life was extremely hazardous. One harvest in six regularly failed, bringing in its train starvation, sickness and death. Poor food, hygiene and lack of medical knowledge meant that epidemics were common. In London alone they accounted for thirty per cent of reported deaths. In the 150 years up to 1665, there were only a dozen years in which the metropolis was free from plague.

If you were lucky enough to survive disease, you had to run the gauntlet of contemporary medicine. Not only were there very few qualified doctors, the ones who did practise were woefully ignorant by modern standards. Lacking adequate theories of disease, they believed that most illnesses were the result of an imbalance between four humours: blood, phlegm, yellow and black bile. Their remedies were equally simple and mistaken: blood-letting, purges and emetics.

When it came to surgery, you were no better off. Without an understanding of anatomy or physiology, the most that surgeons could do was to operate on a limited range of conditions such as broken limbs, parts requiring amputation, and abscesses. Without anaesthetics or even rudimentary anti-infection measures, the mortality rate was high. It should come as no surprise that most sufferers preferred the disease to the treatment.

This was the reality of everyday life without science. The only alternative was religious superstition. Shrines of the saints at places like Glastonbury, Canterbury and Walsingham became objects of pilgrimage to which the sick and desperate would make long and painful journeys in the hope of supernatural healing. At Thomas Becket's shrine alone, some five hundred miracles were alleged to have taken place, while at Bromholm in Norfolk, thirty-nine people were said to have been raised from the dead and twelve cured of blindness. All hocus-pocus, as we now know.

And woe betide you if you failed to venerate the right saints. The sixteenth-century Reformer, William Tyndale, mocked when he wrote that: 'We worship saints for fear lest they should be displeased and angry with us, and plague us or hurt us.' Caustically he went on, 'Who dare deny St Anthony a fleece of wool for fear of his terrible fire, or lest he send the pox among our sheep?'

Such was the state of late medieval England. Trapped in disease, squalor and magic, it had no means of escape until the arrival of science. It was not religion or theology that brought liberation but science. The breakthroughs in improving the lot of ordinary people were the direct result of scientific advance – nothing more. Only when religion lost its grip did genuine progress begin. And what is more, it is science that is achieving similar successes in developing countries today. The World Health Organization and other agencies are triumphing over disease and mortality not by colluding with pre-scientific mumbo-jumbo, but by the persistent application of scientific principles. In the words of Nehru, the first Prime Minister of India after the departure of the British: 'It is science alone that can solve the problems of hunger and poverty, of insanitation and illiteracy, of superstition and deadening custom . . . The future belongs to science and those who make friends with science.'

2. *Humanity Come of Age*

If Nehru is right – and agnostics believe he is – to embrace science means embracing humanity's coming of age. Just as children shed their dependence on their parents as they mature into adulthood, so humanity no longer needs religion and magic for infantile security. We have grown up at last. We can do without religion to tuck us up at night. We are learning to encounter the universe without help. In the words of Freud, 'Scientific knowledge is the only road which can lead us to a knowledge of a reality outside ourselves.' We should rejoice in it.

This coming of age is well expressed by the biologist, Richard Dawkins. 'We no longer have to resort to superstition,' he says, 'when faced with deep problems: Is there a meaning to life? What are we for? What is man?' Instead, we can now discover truth through science, for 'Darwin made it possible to be an intellectually fulfilled atheist.' Or, to quote physicist Peter Atkins: 'We are almost there. Complete knowledge is just within our grasp. Comprehension is moving across the face of the earth like a sunrise.'

The reason for such confidence lies not in switching from one crutch (religion) to another (science). Rather, it springs from the proven ability of the scientific method to find out how things work and to guarantee progress. Unlike religious speculation, which is based on nothing more than blind faith in the unknown and unprovable, science is not satisfied until it has rationally established by observation and investigation how things actually are. Dawkins can boast in his atheism precisely because the evidence for evolution is now so compelling that God is made redundant.

The same point can be made across the range of human endeavour. According to the renowned humanist, Kit Mouat, 'From biology to botany, anthropology to anatomy, sociology to psychology, there is no aspect of life in which science of one sort or another has not something invaluable to contribute.' Or as J. D. Bernal wrote in 1939, 'Already we have in the practice of science the prototype for all common human action.'

Since Bernal and Mouat, the advance of scientific understanding has been phenomenal. We have seen how the prospect of a Theory of Everything is now held to be a realistic possibility. Cosmologists, physicists and mathematicians are now openly talking about understanding not just the origins of the universe – as if that were not astounding enough – but of developing a theory that will explain the whole of reality. Here is Peter Atkins again: 'There is nothing that cannot be understood . . . nothing that cannot be explained . . . everything is extraordinarily simple.' John Wheeler writes: 'Physics is a magic window . . . Its scope is immensely greater than we once realised. We are no longer satisfied with insights only into particles, or fields of force, or geometry, or even space or time. Today we demand of physics some understanding of existence itself.'

Science is able make such a claim because it offers credible explanations across the whole of life. This is why both God and faith must be reckoned to be outmoded. A few examples will serve to illustrate this.

When we turn to *modern physics*, we find that the workings of the cosmos have been laid bare. Quasars, black holes and singularities have entered common parlance, while we now have a much clearer idea of reality at the subatomic level. The world of protons, quarks, gluons, space-time foam and superstrings beckons. Our Theory of Everything extends from the reaches of the universe to the world of the quantum. And God is irrelevant to it all.

Then there is *cosmology*, a branch of modern physics which offers an almost unbelievable insight into the first moments of the universe. Using evidence from astronomy and high-energy physics, it is possible to create a plausible reconstruction of cosmic history back to the first three minutes of existence, fifteen billion years ago (yes, the first three minutes!) This is nothing short of astounding. We do not need to resort to the crude myths of Genesis or the dogmatism of fundamentalist creationists to answer the question how we got here. We can give a reasoned answer without reference to a divinity. Indeed, if Stephen Hawking and others are right about the nature of space and time, we can accept the plausibility of a self-generating universe. There is no need of God; mathematical equations will do instead.

Likewise, *evolutionary theory* is fully capable of supplying a complete history of life, from its appearance in microscopic form some three billion years ago to the complexities of the contemporary human brain. Dawkins can remain intellectually satisfied because, as in cosmology, God is no longer necessary. Evolution has supplanted God. Moreover, the discovery of DNA and subsequent research means that not only do we now understand the most basic component of life but we are also able to manipulate it. Genetic engineering is no longer science fantasy but scientific fact.

But science does not stop with the physical sciences. In the human sciences we similarly discover that it is possible (and plausible) to do away with God. Freud exposed the innermost workings of the human psyche such that supernaturalism could be ruled out as an explanation of behaviour. Neither demons nor the Holy Ghost need be invoked any longer. Explicitly modelling his methods upon biology and physics, Freud confidently argued that this would 'put us in a position to establish psychology on foundations similar to those of any other science'. Psychology since has continued to operate on the assumption that it offers explanations every bit as scientific as those offered in the physical sciences. Once again, religion is redundant.

3. Reason not Religion

What are the hallmarks of this scientific method that has revolutionized the world and done away with the need for God? They can be narrowed down to three: reason, observation and experimentation. What makes science distinctive is its relentless pursuit of truth through the application of human reason to observation and investigation of phenomena until their workings are made plain. Reason absolutely refuses to rely on half-baked prejudices inherited from the past. Instead it is ruthless in its determination to get at facts rather than opinions. Objectivity is everything. Only such a method is sufficient for a humanity intent on life without dependence on mythical god-figures. We can echo C. H. Waddington wholeheartedly in his insistence that: 'Science by itself is able to provide mankind with a way of life which is, firstly, self-consistent and harmonious, and, secondly, free for the exercise of that objective reason on which our material progress depends.'

The triumph of scientific reason is thus the crowning glory of the modern age. When we compare our knowledge of the world with the laughable beliefs of medievalism, we are amazed that religion took so long to die. Take, for example, the idea of cause and effect. This is probably the single most important insight of the scientific revolution. Without it, we should be stuck in the Dark Ages. Yet when we look at what medieval thinkers actually believed we are astonished that they could hold to such nonsense. According to the teachings of Aristotle (whose science formed the basis of medievalism) causes must be understood in terms of purpose. Ask the question, 'Why does a rock fall to the ground when dropped from a height?' and the answer would be 'Because the purpose of everything is to seek its natural resting place and the natural place for a rock is on the ground.' Nowadays we would explain such a phenomenon in terms of gravity-induced cause and effect. But for the medieval mind, the key to scientific understanding lay in the notion of purpose.

This, in turn, was set within a much larger picture of God's purposes for the universe. Each natural event was assumed to fit into the grand scheme of things in conformity with God's will. Therefore, the primary task of science was to discover how particular phenomena were related to the overarching divine purpose.

When we compare such an approach with science as we know it today, it quickly becomes obvious how revolutionary the rise of modern scientific method actually was. Instead of looking for divine purposes behind events, scientific thinkers such as Galileo, Kepler and Newton insisted that science need be concerned only with descriptive explanation. To quote Ian Barbour, 'Galileo asked not *why* objects fall, but *how* they fall.'

Allied to this was the belief in observation and experimentation. Greek and medieval science had made room for some degree of observation but this was to illustrate rational first principles rather than to discover how things worked. The scientific revolution, on the other hand, put experimentation at its centre. Only by means of persistent and repeated experiments could patterns within events be observed out of which general laws of nature could be developed.

This all seems so elementary to us that we marvel at how science could have been viewed otherwise. Yet if it were not for the breakthrough in method just described, we should still be seeking explanations in terms of cosmic purpose rather than causal laws. In other words, we would be stranded in the Middle Ages.

4. *Religious Prejudice Rules OK*

History is littered with instances of the Church's resistance to science. Whether we are talking of the rejection of Galileo in the seventeenth century or the condemnation of Darwin in the nineteenth, the story is the same. The development of modern science has been fought by the Church at every turn. Even in the late 1990s, at the end of the millennium, there are still those so controlled by blind prejudice that no scientific evidence is admissible if it conflicts with fundamentalist dogma. When, in August 1996, NASA scientists announced that they believed they had found traces of life on a meteorite originating from Mars, religious bigots could be heard dismissing the claim out of hand. If religion had had its way when the scientific revolution began, we should still believe that the earth lay at the centre of the universe and that the sun orbited around us because human beings were the most important creatures in creation. Likewise, we would date the earth's origin at 4004 BC and expect the ground to be the natural resting place for objects when they fall because they have a homing instinct for the centre of the earth. This would be tragic if it were not so pathetic.

We need not go into all the other fallacies to which we would be committed if the Church had prevailed: creation according to a literal reading of Genesis; the impossibility of 'unnatural' flight ('if God's purpose had been for us to fly he would have given us wings'); space travel; modern medicine – the list is endless. It is surprising the Church has any adherents at all.

But what is even more appalling is that the Church has consistently sought to stamp out scientific advance and persecute its proponents just because they disagreed with the dogma of the times and threatened the power of the institution. Galileo, for example, was forced by the Pope to retract his *findings* (not just his views) at the age of seventy in the most humiliating public terms. Condemned to life imprisonment, he was made to deny the convictions he had established scientifically for more than twenty years: 'I, Galileo, being in my seventieth year, being a prisoner and on my knees, and before your Eminences, having before my eyes the Holy Gospel which I touch with my hands, abjure, curse, and detest the error and heresy of the movement of the earth.'

The Galileo affair, of course, was about more than science. At its heart lay ecclesiastical power politics and institutional fear. Nevertheless, nothing could illustrate more powerfully the attractions of agnosticism. For openness and resistance to dogma are its hallmarks, whereas intolerance and closed mindedness are the chief characteristics of religion. The Church has always been the enemy of science and scientific truth. It is no coincidence that as science has risen so religion has fallen. And as science continues to expand our knowledge of the universe, so the outdated pretensions of faith will evaporate like mist in the noonday sun.

Conclusion

In this chapter we have seen how science and religious belief are essentially incompatible. In every important respect, science must be regarded as the royal road to knowledge because science alone can:

- give us an accurate picture of how the world works;
- give humanity control over its own destiny;
- meet the material needs of the world;
- back up its claims with empirical proof;
- bring coherence and meaning to the facts of the universe as we know them;
- offer hope for the future;
- provide a philosophy for humanity come of age; and
- free us from superstition and magic.

Religion offers none of these things. Consequently, agnostics can take to heart Waddington's belief that: 'At the present time, only science has the vigour and authority of achievement to make these highest human values captivate men's hearts and minds.'

2
The Chastening of Science

Modern man turns towards science, or rather against it, now seeing its terrible capacity to destroy not only bodies but the soul itself.

Jacques Monod

By the end of the nineteenth century, optimism about scientific progress had triumphed over all that stood in its path. It was assumed that such progress would continue indefinitely. Indeed, despite two world wars and the advent of the nuclear bomb, it could still be found as late as the 1960s. Harold Wilson, Leader of the British Labour Party – soon to be Prime Minister – speaking in revivalist terms to his party conference in 1963, could triumphally proclaim: 'In all our plans for the future, we are re-defining and we are restating our Socialism in terms of the scientific revolution . . . In the Cabinet room and the boardroom alike those charged with the control of our affairs must be ready to think and to speak in the language of our scientific age.'

Such was the power of the scientific world-view. The appeal to science as the key to the future good of humanity had become so deeply embedded that to question it would have sounded heretical. Indeed, we need to remember that it was at this time exactly that theologians in the West were proclaiming the 'death of God' and the advent of 'secular religion'. In Mary Midgley's words, science had come to be seen not merely as a method for discovering facts but instead as 'a whole myth, a philosophical conception of the world and the forces within it, directly related to the meaning of human life.' Science offered 'a vast interpretative scheme which could shape the spiritual life, a faith by which people might live.'

Yet the triumphalism of our agnostic of Chapter 1 has in fact been dealt a series of hammer blows at the very same time it has appeared to carry all before it. In this chapter we shall see exactly what these blows have been. But as we do so, we shall discover a strange phenomenon. The critique we assemble will not be supplied by religionists, for that would be too predictable. Rather, we shall see that some of the fiercest attacks have come from agnostics themselves. For those who still cherish hopes that science can offer the answer to everything, this may come as something of a shock.

Ironically, the very success of science we noted in the last chapter has also thrown light on its failure. The belief in science as a total world-view can no longer be sustained. This is partly for pragmatic reasons, but it is also because the intellectual confidence which drove such a belief has been undermined by unrelenting radical questioning.

The Double-Edged Sword

The selfsame scientific and technological mindset that gave us economic, social and medical progress has also given us nuclear weapons, environmental disasters, the gulags and the Holocaust. It is no coincidence that the most dreadful regimes of the twentieth century – Stalin's Russia and Hitler's Germany – both laid claim to science as the basis of their philosophies. For Stalin it was scientific socialism; for Hitler, a blend of social Darwinism and quasi-scientific theories of race and eugenics. The result in each case was the same: a search for ever-increasingly efficient ways to liquidate opponents and (in Hitler's case) the so-called 'subhuman' races. We need to remember that the myth of Aryan superiority was based upon the so-called Nazi 'science of race' and that the elimination of Jews, homosexuals and Slavs followed from pseudo-scientific theories of eugenics.

But it was not just a matter of ideologies. The horrors of the extermination camps, whether in Soviet Siberia or in German-occupied Poland, would simply not have been possible without the triumph of scientific technology. Although despots throughout history have dreamed of eliminating their enemies, only in the mid-twentieth century have they come to possess the means to do so on such an unprecedented scale. Auschwitz was the ultimate symbol of the triumph of industrial know-how.

In reply, of course, it could be argued that this was hardly the fault of science itself. The gulags and the concentration camps were the invention of evil human minds. They did not happen simply because science had advanced far enough to make them feasible. Science in itself was neutral; it was twisted human beings who perverted it.

But, despite the apparent reasonableness of such an argument, it cannot stand up to scrutiny. Those who created the exact science of extermination were well aware of what they were doing. Like the makers of the atomic bomb, they could not plead ignorance of the consequences of their actions. The cry that it was up to the politicians to decide what to do with the fruits of scientific research and that it was not the job of scientists to make moral judgements amounted to moral abdication. The Holocaust, the gulags and Hiroshima demonstrated once and for all that science could no longer take refuge in 'objectivity'. The fanatical commitment to the fact/value distinction which lay at the heart of rationalist science had proved a disaster. This is hammer blow number one.

But more than this, if anything the distinction had proved too much. For if science is merely instrumental and it is up to humans to determine how to use it, then it cannot supply the kind of total world-view we noted some of its proponents espousing in Chapter 1. The best science can do is to offer a perspective on how the world works from a scientific standpoint. It cannot pronounce upon what to do with such knowledge. Science cannot have it both ways.

Once this is conceded, of course, belief in science as the answer to everything begins to crumble. Room has to be created for non-scientific categories such as morality and aesthetic judgement; and once this happens, the belief in scientific reason as the final and exclusive arbiter of truth is undermined. There turn out to be other kinds of knowledge which are important and which science cannot supply. This is hammer blow number two.

Illusions about Human Nature

But suppose we concede for a moment that science really is neutral, a mere tool in the hands of humans who harness it to whatever set of values they believe in. Then the history of this century suggests that it rests in precarious hands indeed. The optimism of Waddington and Mouat about human nature seems horribly misplaced, while the naive triumphalism of Richard Dawkins appears grotesque. In the light of all that has happened since 1914, to persevere in believing that science can answer all the questions of life is at best delusional and at worst catastrophic. One has only to look around the world at present, let alone historically, to see that for all the good that science has achieved, it has been instrumental in creating some of the worst nightmares imaginable.

Once again, we need to remember that this criticism can be mounted without the aid of religion or theology. One does not have to be a religionist to see that the boast of science to have separated the discovery of facts from the realm of values (which was supposed to open up the way for the triumph of progress over superstition) has proved illusory. It could only appear to work in societies which retained a strong enough bedrock of humane values to underpin technological advance with a moral base. Once such a base had been eroded (as in Soviet Russia or Nazi Germany) the way lay open for science to be used for evil purposes. The fact/value split robbed scientists of any right to argue against research on moral grounds, since for two centuries science had been claiming that by its very nature it was concerned not with subjective beliefs but with objective facts. A moral vacuum thus opened up at the heart of the scientific enterprise into which ideologies of left and right were only too willing to jump.

The implication of this, of course, is that humanity can hardly be said to have come of age. The optimism of an earlier generation of humanists has given way either to the bleak pessimism of existentialists such as Sartre and Camus (for whom life is nothing but a sick joke), or to the amoralism of bureaucratic technocracy. Where optimistic agnostics still exist, they do so on the basis of a leap of faith no less real than that of religious believers. Humanity, therefore, whether considered individualistically or collectively, teeters perpetually on the brink of self-destruction; and no amount of wishful thinking about the nobility of human beings will change that. The optimism of scientistic agnosticism is undermined at every turn by the facts not of the laboratory but of historical experience. This is hammer blow number three.

A Critique from Reason not Religion

These, then, are some of the pragmatic arguments offered against belief in science as the answer to all human questions. The problem for the agnostic of Chapter 1, though, is made even worse when we turn to the central claim made for scientific method, namely that it alone provides us with privileged access to truth and reality.

This view has been held by scientists and the general public for such a long time that it is hard for us to think critically about it. The result has been a kind of myopia in which we see only those things which our limited vision enables us to see. So it is at this point that we need to look at some of the leading critiques offered by a number of agnostic philosophers. So significant are these and so central to the debate about science and religious faith that we must spend some time dwelling upon them.

The Argument Set Out

The optimistic view of science rests upon a number of assumptions:

1. There exists an objective reality, independent of our wishes or thoughts, which can be discovered and analysed by the methods of investigative science.
2. Scientific methods themselves are objective in that they do not depend upon the whims of the scientist investigator for their validity; they arise from an absolute belief among the scientific community that rational inquiry based on observation, experimentation and evaluation of results will lead to true knowledge. Another way of putting this is to say that anyone, in principle, can use these methods provided they have the necessary understanding and skills, whatever their personal beliefs.
3. If we want to know about the true nature of reality, it is science that is best placed to show us. The world (or the cosmos for that matter) is most accurately described in the language of science.
4. Scientific method is universal. It cuts across cultures and societies so that what is true, say, in Japan is also true in France. If a scientist conducts an experiment

in Asia on Monday, she will get the same result from an identical experiment conducted under identical conditions in Europe on Tuesday. The laws of science are universally true.

5. The kind of knowledge yielded by scientific investigation is somehow the truest sort of knowledge we can get. Other kinds, such as aesthetic, moral or intuitive 'knowledge' may not even be candidates for knowledge at all since they are based on subjective feelings or opinions rather than verifiable facts.

Taken together, these five assumptions add up to a pretty powerful package which has formed the basis for agnostic and atheist critiques of religion up to the present day. They also control the mindset of much popular science fiction, especially as viewed on TV and film, as the success of such series as *Star Trek* shows. Yet in recent years, all these assumptions have been thrown into question. None has remained immune from critical scrutiny and none has survived in its original unqualified form. In short, the belief in the privileged status of science as the exclusive route to true knowledge has been so severely undermined as to be near to collapse from within. And this has all arisen without reference to God, religion or theology. There has been nothing short of a revolution in thinking about science. It is to this we must now turn.

1. Objectively Neutral Scientific Method is a Fraud

In 1962, the historian and philosopher of science,Thomas Kuhn, published a book which shattered the illusions of scientists and public alike. His basic thesis was that the popular view of science as an ever-increasing body of certain knowledge gained by painstaking, step-by-step research was false. Such a picture (argued Kuhn) adequately describes what might be called 'normal science' – the day-to-day incremental advances in knowledge. But it completely fails to describe the kind of breakthroughs that have led to great leaps forward in understanding.

Why was this so? At this point Kuhn introduced the notion of paradigms. By this he meant that scientific research at any given moment is governed by accepted ways of looking at the world and accepted procedures for doing so. Scientists carry out their work within a consensus about what is true (and what is not) on the basis of tried and tested methods: hence the image of the scientist in a white coat carefully conducting experiments in the laboratory to add bit by bit to the sum of human knowledge.

Kuhn accepted this characterization as true for much of scientific research – hence the term 'normal science'. The problem arises, however, when we look at how historic breakthroughs are made. These occur, he says, when 'normal science' can no longer account for the phenomena under investigation. That is to say, the paradigm which has hitherto worked, no longer does. It cannot explain the evidence in question. The facts can no longer be accounted for by the traditional way of looking at things (Galileo or Darwin, for example, both challenged accepted paradigms).

So what happens at this point? According to Kuhn, a new paradigm, a new way of looking at reality, has to be formed. There occurs what he calls a 'paradigm shift' as the old paradigm is busted open by the new, and a breakthrough in understanding takes place.

But – and herein lies the rub – such revolutions do not happen because the scientific community is moving in their direction according to accepted procedures ('normal science'). Almost always, the revolutionary proposal is fiercely resisted by scientists until the old paradigm can survive no more. The full weight of the scientific establishment is brought to bear on the revolutionary making their proposal, in a determined effort to invalidate it or make it fit with the current consensus.

If this is true – and Kuhn illustrates his claim with a

series of historical examples such as the revolution that followed Newton – then we are faced with a bizarre picture. The popular image of science as a coolly rational and dispassionate accumulation of indisputable facts turns out to be a myth. It may be adequate to portray small, uncontroversial advances but it totally fails at the level of major advances. Indeed, such revolutions are achieved only by denying whatever paradigm is endorsed by normal science.

Thirteen years later in 1975, Paul Feyerabend offered an even more radical view. Since Kuhn's *The Structure of Scientific Revolutions*, the debate among the scientific community had centred on how far new paradigms are formed by old paradigms simply incorporating new theories until a new paradigm is brought into being. On this view, at least some breakthroughs occur not by pulling down existing paradigms in a single revolutionary act but by gradually absorbing new insights until a new way of seeing things comes into being. In other words, paradigm shifts occur as much by a process of evolution as by revolution.

Feyerabend, however, would have none of this. In his book, *Against Method*, he went further than Kuhn to claim that the truly great breakthroughs have come about only by deliberately discarding what went before, not by assimilating it in any way whatsoever. When Copernicus presented his view that the Sun rather than the Earth lay at the centre of the planetary system, he was not building upon the previous view – he was destroying it. There could be no accommodation between the old paradigm and the new; one simply overturned the other. Similarly, when quantum theory became accepted in this century, it did so not by accepting classical atomic theory but by denying it. Hence the persistent refusal by Einstein to endorse quantum views.

But Feyerabend went even beyond this. He explicitly argued that scientists must challenge their most cherished paradigms by deliberately thinking in contrast to their previously accepted ways. 'Normal science' could only *prevent* breakthroughs – it could not engender them. Only when they are liberated from the constraints of 'normal' scientific method can scientists achieve genuine paradigm change. They must 'invent a new conceptual system that suspends, or clashes with the most carefully observed observational results, confounds the most plausible theoretical principles, and introduces perceptions that cannot form part of the existing perceptual world'.

This was radical stuff indeed! And what's more, argued Feyerabend, scientists must be prepared to think imaginatively rather than analytically if they are to achieve genuinely creative results. They must deliberately use thinking far outside the normal scientific paradigms. The incrementalist view must be dumped.

> There is no idea, however ancient and absurd, that is not capable of improving our knowledge. The whole history of thought is absorbed into science and is used for improving every single theory. Nor is political interference rejected. It may be needed to overcome the chauvinism of science that resists alternatives to the status quo.

This is a far cry from the measured progress of rational, step-by-step procedure.

This 'scepticism from the inside' exemplified by Kuhn and Feyerabend formed but part of a wider reaction against what some have labelled 'scientism' – the belief that science is or can be the only complete explanation of reality. If space permitted, we would also have to consider the writings of Karl Popper and Michael Polanyi. The crucial point to grasp, however, is that they have all turned upside down the way we look at the scientific enterprise. Scientific method can no longer be seen as the outcome of impersonal, unbiased, objective thinking which is universally applicable, but instead must be seen as the product of culture-bound communities of individuals shaped by their predispositions, histories and prejudices. We could scarcely get further away from the assumptions of our optimistic agnostic.

Moreover, in this respect, the scientific community is no different from the Church. Both are institutions controlled by dominant paradigms; both are run by establishment elites who have a vested interest in preserving the status quo since it legitimates their own power; both are incredibly resistant to paradigm changes until they are forced on them; and both operate with a series of hidden (and not so hidden) prejudices which lead them to rule out opposition. So much for the objectivity presupposed by the popular view of science.

2. There Are No Secure Foundations for Knowing Anything

Classical science (the kind that our agnostic of the previous chapter puts his faith in) assumed that it was possible (at least in principle) to render the universe naked by the application of scientific method. We could therefore rest secure in the knowledge that eventually everything would be explained by the immutable and unstoppable power of scientific investigation. This was the foundation of true knowledge and progress.

But all that has changed. If there is no such thing as objective scientific method, it follows that we can never be sure we have discovered more than the products of our own cultural viewpoint. We may believe we are seeing the universe as it really is, but who is to decide whether we are wearing the correct pair of spectacles or merely looking in a cultural mirror?

If Kuhn, Feyerabend and others are to be taken seriously, no assurance of the kind claimed by the popular view of science can ever exist. Because of its embeddedness in particular cultural forms, Western science can never be objective, however much scientists may think it is.

Therefore, what we think of as knowledge may be no more than a reflection of our own making. It is as if we were to look down a deep well expecting to see the bottom but only ever seeing it through the reflection of our own faces in the water.

In reply, of course, it might be said that we can verify or falsify our scientific suppositions by empirical experiment. But even this offers no escape from the relativist trap. For not even experiments are immune from contamination by cultural assumptions and beliefs. The way in which an experiment is conducted, observations recorded and interpreted and conclusions drawn will depend on the procedures used and the assumptions held by the investigator. A scientist who has already made up her mind, for example, not to believe that the medical condition ME has a physiological basis, but is all in the mind, is unlikely to be persuaded by evidence to the contrary. Any findings which might contradict her belief will be disregarded or reinterpreted by incorporating them within her sceptical framework.

Consequently, the scientist can never have access to raw reality. She must always interpret such 'reality' by means of paradigms and presuppositions which themselves are culturally generated and conditioned. Since she may well not be aware that these operate at the subconscious level, the scientist will think she is being objective. In fact, she will be working with a set of assumptions every bit as much as any religious believer does.

Paradigms, of course, are not confined to scientists. We use them all the time. The point is that whereas the rationalist view of science presupposed that science was free from conditioning, operating on neutral ground as it were, it is now clear that no such ground exists. All is relative, nothing is fixed. All that once seemed solid has melted into air.

This is a neat argument which overturns traditional

assumptions about science. We can no longer hope to discover the cosmos as it really is. The most we can do is to come up with a provisional picture of how it might be, given certain assumptions. We cannot speak of science as if it were the royal road to ultimate knowledge but only as a fragile interpretation of those segments of reality we can observe – and a culture-trapped interpretation at that. Knowledge, far from being the solid rock of classical science, becomes a mound of shifting sand. There is no room left for the certainty of the optimistic agnostic who thought he had done away with the perilous and unscientific claims of religion. Everything is suddenly much more tenuous.

3. Objective Truth Does Not Exist

Enlightenment faith in science equated truth with only one kind of knowledge – that which could be proved scientifically. Claims which could not be grounded in empirically observable reality were simply not candidates for truth. The only kind of truth that counted was that which could be shown to correspond to actual states of affairs. Thus the notion of empirically guaranteed objective truth was born.

But such a notion was flawed from the start. If, as we have seen, there is no such thing as uninterpreted reality, but merely differing pictures of reality conditioned by culture and prior assumptions, then the distinction between fact and value is undermined. Attempts to describe phenomena in a neutral language free from contamination will fail, simply because no such language exists. The way we think, form concepts and express ourselves is conditioned by the culture in which we live. Descriptions of the world will always contain hidden (or explicit) metaphysical beliefs, whether these are the beliefs of Amazonian animists who believe that trees possess spirits or the beliefs of late-twentieth-century Western societies who ridicule such 'primitive' ideas. Both claim to offer pictures of reality which contradict each other. Both cannot be true.

The scientific world-view attempts to solve the problem by appealing to empirical evidence, or lack of it. 'How can trees possess spirits', its proponents say, 'when there is no empirical evidence that such beings exist?' 'But who are you to say they do not? replies the Amazonian. 'You have not truly searched for them because you had made up your mind from the start. Be ready to feel the spirits and you will.'

We do not have to believe in tree spirits to get the point. How are we to choose between rival claims to truth when all claims (including those of science) are culturally determined? This is the fundamental dilemma.

The rationalist scientific project, therefore, was founded on a myth. The supposedly objective language of science has turned out to be riddled with prior concepts, assumptions and values. The bold, defiant claim of science to offer privileged access to truth turns out to be a mirage.

Conclusion

We have seen how there has been a revolution in thinking about science. The self-confident days of rationalism have gone, to be replaced by deep scepticism about the claims of science to have unlocked the secrets of the cosmos or to have discovered reality in all its fullness. In this revolution, agnostics have been far more prominent than religionists. Indeed, it might fairly be said that the organized religions of the West have been too busy trying to accommodate themselves to the alleged 'truths' of science to have noticed that such claims have become outmoded. The cultural movement known as postmodernism has raised far more radically sceptical questions about science than religious protagonists could ever have hoped to get away with. The greatest critics of our sure-footed agnostic of Chapter 1 are his fellow agnostics.

3

Science and Faith Revisited

> *Even when all possible scientific questions have been answered, the problems of human life remain completely untouched.*
>
> Ludwig Wittgenstein

The agnostics have had a fair run for their money. It is time for the religionist to respond. One possible response would be that the postmodern critique has proved so devastating that the humiliation of scientific triumphalism is complete. However, this would be unwise. For post-modernism is no respecter of world-views; and it can make exactly the same critique of religion as of science. From a postmodernist perspective, both are simply standing in the same queue in search of credibility. The question is whether there is any hope for restoring it to either. I shall argue there is. Science and faith must stand or fall together.

To see how this is the case, we shall look at a number of convergences between the methods and claims of science and those of religion. We shall see that far from being opponents, they bear remarkable similarities. Moreover, it should be noted that almost all the quotations in what follows come from non-religious sources, A. N. Whitehead and John Polkinghorne being the exceptions.

1. Both Religion and Science Believe in a Real Universe

Postmodernism is resolute in its claim that all knowledge

is culture-relative. Yet although this is partially true, it is not the whole truth. Everyday experience shows us that many of the working assumptions of 'normal science' fit not just one culture but all. The jumbo jet that takes off in Thailand and lands in Australia obeys the same physical 'laws' in both countries. The fact that I am typing this in England and a postmodernist philosopher could be doing likewise in China using the same kind of computer illustrates that some realities, at least, are independent of social context. Both I and my Chinese counterpart will use the same operating instructions and expect the same results. Our respective machines will not function differently simply because we are in different parts of the world.

This all seems so obvious that it makes us wonder whether the postmodern critique has been overdone. Yet Kuhn's point about paradigms still holds. History demonstrates that within science as within religion (or any other world-view), the way we look at things is governed by our overarching assumptions and canons of belief.

So what we need to address are world-views. And here religion and science surprisingly make an identical claim: that reality exists independent of the human mind and human cultures and is open to investigation. When faced with the view that reality is somehow constructed rather than given, both religion and science make the same point: that reality is 'out there' ready to be discovered.

In both disciplines, of course, we encounter reality by means of interpreting it. What we 'see' is coloured by the ways our minds work and the prior assumptions we bring to bear. But this does not mean that interpretation is everything. We may end up debating whether particular interpretations are valid; but underlying such debate is the belief that it is possible to get at reality rather than mere interpretations of it.

This is a complex philosophical question. But the basic point is simple: science and religion both believe in the existence of independent reality and stake their credibility on this claim. Moreover, they both hold that their primary task is to explore such reality. The scientist carries out her work in the belief that the structures of the human mind in some way correspond to the structures of the real world: that she can investigate a phenomenon, can trust that her faculties will give her access to it and that her description of it will give genuine insight into its nature.

Likewise, the religious believer assumes that God or some kind of spiritual reality exists and that it is possible to find him or it. Human beings are constituted such that they can (with divine help) discover God and gain some – albeit limited – understanding. In short, both scientists and religionists believe in access to an independent reality which is not purely a matter of cultural construction.

At this point, the sceptic might object: 'All this talk about independent reality begs the question. Scientists can point to observable phenomena to prove their existence. Religionists can't.' This is a common objection, but one which brings us, perhaps surprisingly, to a second convergence.

2. Both Science and Religion Deal in Unobservables

One of the biggest fallacies in the debate between science and religion is to think that science is concerned only with the supposedly 'real' world of what can be observed, whereas religion deals with the speculative vagaries of the 'spiritual' realm which by definition cannot be observed. From this it is usually argued that science is superior because it is able to verify its claims by pointing to empirical evidence.

Nothing could be further from the truth. Such a crude stereotype belongs to a bygone age. The fact is that vast tracts of modern science consist of speculation about unobservables the existence of which is wholly a matter of deduction and inference rather than direct observation.

Take what is known as the New Physics, for example. The world of quantum theory is completely unobservable. In order to formulate hypotheses about what takes place at the subatomic level, physicists have to rely entirely on mathematical and logical deductions. There is simply no way of observing (and therefore of verifying) the invisible particles that are presumed to make up this level of reality. Nothing can be certified: everything is a matter of assumption. In his book, *Serious Talk*, John Polkinghorne, former Professor of Physics at Cambridge, puts it like this:

> [Quantum theory] was invented to describe the behaviour of atoms, and it has proved consistently successful in all its applications . . . We use it now to think about the behaviour of quarks and gluons, systems that are at least *a hundred million times smaller than atoms*. That is a very impressive record of achievement. But the paradox is this: that though we can use it, though we know how to do the sums, and though the sums always seem to give us the right answers, we do not understand the theory. We do not know what is going on. (p.17)

Those schooled in the popular view of science find this hard to accept. 'Surely,' they say, 'scientists must be able to verify and quantify these phenomena? If they can't, how can it be science?'

The short answer is that the common-sense view of science as having to do with only that which is observable and precisely explicable has collapsed. Modern physics deals every day with the unobservable and immeasurable. It cannot see the world of the atom but it knows it is there. What is more, in quantum mechanics, it appears that unless we are prepared to abandon common sense we shall not come to grips with it at all. In the words of Niels Bohr, the founder of quantum physics: 'Anyone who is not shocked by quantum theory has not understood it.'

This is not the place to go into details. The interested

reader should consult the list for further reading at the end of the book. Suffice it to say that although its effects can be measured to some extent, quantum physics is based totally on the unobservable. Yet its components are still presumed to have a real existence. They are not mere fancies. Indeed, as Paul Davies, formerly Professor of Mathematical Physics at the University of Adelaide and now Professor of Natural Philosophy, points out in his book, *God and the New Physics*: 'quantum theory is primarily a practical branch of physics, and as such is brilliantly successful.' Among its fruits are the laser, the electron microscope and nuclear power. It is a routine part of engineering and is 'in its everyday application, a very down-to-earth subject with a vast body of supporting evidence, not only from commercial gadgetry, but from careful and delicate scientific experiments'.

What, then, are we to make of this? It seems we have a crucial branch of physics (itself the model science which other sciences historically have sought to emulate) based on an inability to conform to the criteria of observability and explicability. On the popular view of science, we might reasonably wonder whether it should count as a true science at all!

A similar problem arises with cosmology, that branch of modern physics that deals with the origins and future of the universe. After decades of obscurity, it has now entered popular awareness through the writings of scientists such as Stephen Hawking. Here speculation runs rife. How did the universe begin? How will it end? How many universes are there? Answers to these and many other questions are as much matters of faith as of fact. By definition, the Big Bang was unobservable by us (although traces of it linger on in the form of radiation from which scientists have deduced both that the Big Bang happened and how long ago). Yet it is now generally accepted as the way the universe began, despite the fact that no one observed it and that we have only indirect evidence and inference.

Even more bizarre are some of the wilder speculations about the existence of multiple universes existing in parallel dimensions – a theme made popular by science fiction. Here is how Bryce de Witt, a pioneer of this theory puts it: 'Our universe must be viewed as constantly splitting into a stupendous number of branches . . . Every quantum transition taking place on every star, in every galaxy, in every remote corner of the universe is splitting our local world into myriad copies of itself. Here is schizophrenia with a vengeance!'

Indeed. Yet respectable scientists support such speculations. David Deutsch is a research fellow at the Department of Astrophysics at Oxford and at the University of Texas at Austin. Asked about why he accepts the many universes idea, he replies that 'the theory which predicts them is the simplest interpretation of quantum theory, and we believe quantum theory because of its enormous experimental success.' Similarly, Paul Davies and J. Brown contend that the existence of multiple universes

> would provide an easy explanation for the formidable range of mysterious 'coincidences' and 'accidents of nature' found in physics, biology and cosmology . . . If the many-universes theory were correct, the seemingly contrived organisation of the cosmos would be no mystery. We could safely assume that all possible arrangements of matter and energy are represented somewhere among the infinite ensemble of universes.

It is important to grasp what is happening here in the name of science. The scientists are not saying that they have observed these phenomena. Indeed, in their view it is impossible to do so since 'the splitting process is quite unobservable.' Instead of hard evidence, therefore, of the kind demanded by those who have criticized religion as unscientific, they offer a combination of inference, extrapolation and speculation – in short, they indulge in precisely the same sort of activity which a previous generation of scientists regarded as the very reason why religion should be dismissed. This is deeply ironic. To quote the philosopher of science, Karl Popper, 'I am inclined to think that scientific discovery is impossible without faith in ideas which are of a purely speculative kind and sometimes quite hazy; a faith which is quite unwarranted from a scientific point of view.'

3. Materialism Is Dead

We tend to think of materialism in terms of acquiring more and more possessions – a partner to greed. But that is only one of its meanings. In scientific and philosophical terms, materialism is the doctrine that only matter truly exists and that every other attempt to describe reality (as spirit or mind, for example) is false. When analysed carefully, everything that happens can be explained as the outcome of material forces. There is no other dimension to reality. Matter rules.

This was the dominant scientific paradigm, or way of interpreting reality, for two centuries. Its heyday ran from the time of Isaac Newton to the mid-twentieth century and can be found in popular science even now. It continues to underlie the alleged 'incompatibility' between science and faith.

Yet, as many scientists now recognize, materialism is dead. Its basic premise – that the universe is nothing but a mechanism – has been rejected as inadequate. As Paul Davies and John Gribbin point out in their book, *The Matter Myth*, 'increasing numbers of scientists are coming to recognise the limitations of the materialistic view of nature, and to appreciate that there is more to the world than cogs in a gigantic machine.'

Why should this be so? For the simple reason that, as the Austrian philosopher Ludwig Wittgenstein pointed out in the quotation that began this chapter, a version of science which regards things as no more than the movement of atoms on a large or small scale has nothing to say about the central problems of human life. Or in the words of geneticist Jacques Monod, 'Modern man turns toward science, or rather against it, now seeing its terrible capacity to destroy not only bodies but the soul itself.'

In practice, however, whatever materialists might say, human beings refuse to act as if the materialist account were true. We deny that love can be reduced to the activity of electrochemicals in the brain. We don't accept that people are nothing but a collection of basic elements arranged in a particular manner. We live as if we are more than that, as if human beings possess significance which transcends the materialist interpretation. In other words, we acknowledge the realm of the human spirit.

The fundamental flaw in the materialistic view, then, has been its ruthless determination to fit everything into the machine model. In doing so, it has left no room for the things that cannot be measured empirically but which really matter: passion, love, hate, joy, justice, freedom (to name but a few). The price paid for embracing this view of science has been high: an empty, bleak universe robbed of even the smallest iota of freedom or purpose other than to carry on functioning as a gigantic machine; and within this vast mechanism, human beings likewise to be seen as nothing but smaller machines, controlled by the same physical laws (and therefore susceptible to objective scientific analysis).

Little wonder that the second half of the twentieth century has seen a rejection of this view, not only by ordinary people but also by a number of scientists who have found materialism a profoundly unsatisfactory philosophy. They have not simply been convinced by new evidence which throws light on the inadequacies of materialism; they have recognized that in a clockwork universe, there is no room left for other realities.

The issue becomes particularly sharp in the face of moral questions. What makes Nazism wrong and Communism right (or vice versa)? And why should the Holocaust and the gulags have mattered if all moralities are simply the outcomes of material forces thrown up by an impersonal cosmos? Why should individuals such as Jews or dissenters have mattered if they were merely assemblages of chemicals? If we start with the belief that the universe is no more than a giant machine, it becomes impossible to discover a reason from within the universe for objecting to the mass slaughter of human beings. After all, they are merely machines themselves. Let the most efficient machines triumph!

Yet this is not how it has been. The democracies of this century have fought against the evils of Nazism and Communism not just because their own survival was threatened but because they also believed that freedom and justice were values to be defended; that a moral stand had to be taken. But on what logical – as opposed to emotional – grounds can such a belief be upheld? On the mechanistic model it cannot.

4. Science and Religion Are Pushing at the Same Door

Both science and religion are prone to delusions. The central delusion of the materialist/mechanistic model of science was to believe that it had relegated religious questions to the sidelines while it got on with 'real life'. It was confidently assumed that science had effectively done away with religion except as a crutch for the emotionally disabled. The central delusion of religion while this view was popular was to take such claims at face value.

It is therefore interesting that forty years on the tables have been turned. Not only is materialism defunct but some of the most pressing religious questions are being asked by scientists themselves. For the remainder of the chapter we shall explore this development. Our starting point will be not the twentieth but the sixteenth century. For it was this era that gave birth to modern science. There is a deep irony here: the scientific triumphalism of our own times, based on an aggressive and overconfident humanism, owes its inception in part to the religious world-view of four hundred years ago. As Colin Russell, Professor of the History of Science and Technology at the Open University has shown in his book, *Crosscurrents: Interactions Between Science and Faith*, the Christian belief in an orderly creation brought into being by a benevolent Creator offered fertile ground in which science could grow. Combined with a belief in the value of reason as a faculty given by God, this encouraged a spirit of discovery through investigation and thereby paved the way for the so-called 'scientific revolution' of the seventeenth century. (Only subsequently did this become secularized.) In the words of A. N. Whitehead, 'Faith in the possibility of science . . . is an unconscious derivative from medieval theology.'

Moreover, the 'founding fathers' such as Bacon (1561–1626), Boyle (1627–91) and Newton (1642–1727) operated within a world-view which took God for granted. Bacon, for example, warned against reading into nature merely what we think. Instead, he argued, we should seek to discover the orderliness of creation as God himself has established it:

> We will have it that all things are as in our folly we think they should be, not as it seems fittest to the divine wisdom, or as they are found to be in fact . . . we clearly impress the stamp of our own image on the creatures

> and works of God, instead of carefully examining and recognising in them the stamp of the creator himself.

Likewise, Robert Boyle was adamant that only by accepting that the cosmos had been created by God could science proceed:

> Thus the universe being once framed by God and the laws of motion settled and all upheld by his perpetual concourse and general providence; the same philosophy teaches that the phenomena of the world are physically produced by the mechanical properties of the parts of matter, and that they operate upon one another according to mechanical laws.

The scientific endeavour, therefore, owes something to religion – Christianity in particular. By the middle of the present century, however, its roots had been lost. Secularized science seemed to rule the day. Now even that has changed as increasingly scientists are discovering that ultimate questions of meaning, purpose and value (the very things science is supposed to leave to religion) cannot be avoided.

The impulse behind this shift has been our old friend, quantum theory. It is no coincidence that it is the physicists who are now pushing at the door of theology – or, to be more precise, are pushing at the same door that theology has been pushing against for millennia. The high-energy physicist, Fritjof Capra, for example, in his book, *The Tao of Physics*, explores the similarities between modern physics and the Eastern mystical tradition. His exposition of what has been termed 'quantum mysticism' is a serious attempt to expose the hollowness of materialistic/mechanistic philosophy, and to replace it with a synthesis of science and Eastern religion which is far more subtle and open to the realm of the spirit than earlier scientific thinking could ever have been.

Similarly, Paul Davies, although not holding any particular religious allegiance, nonetheless finds himself attracted by mysticism as providing a way to a spiritual reality closed to the methods of science. He is sceptical about the ability of science to yield final knowledge since it does not possess the ability to do so: 'in the end, a rational explanation for the world in the sense of a closed and complete system of logical truths is almost certainly impossible.' Consequently, 'If we wish to progress beyond, we have to embrace a different concept of "understanding" from that of rational explanation. Possibly the mystical path is a way to such an understanding.'

Such an admission from a renowned physicist would have been unthinkable a generation ago. It is a measure of how far the science and religion debate has travelled that a scientist of Davies' stature can further go on to say, 'I have never had a mystical experience myself, but I keep an open mind about the value of such experiences. Maybe they provide the only route beyond the limits to which science and philosophy can take us, the only possible path to the Ultimate.'

In the heyday of scientific atheism or agnosticism (not that many years ago), Davies would have been disowned as a crank for saying this. Yet the fact is that he articulates a growing awareness that science and religion, far from being incompatible, are embarked upon similar quests – to discover the truth about reality in all its dimensions: 'Science may explain all the processes whereby the universe evolves its own destiny, but that still leaves room for there to be a meaning behind existence.' And, moreover, he has a clear message for his sceptical colleagues:

> Should we adopt the approach of the pragmatic atheist who is content to take the universe as given, and get on with cataloguing its properties? There is no doubt that many scientists are opposed temperamentally to any

> form of metaphysical, let alone mystical arguments. They are scornful of the notion that there might exist a God, or even an impersonal creative principle or ground of being that would underpin reality and render its contingent aspects less starkly arbitrary. *Personally I do not share their scorn.* Although many metaphysical and theistic theories seem contrived or childish, they are not obviously more absurd than the belief that the universe exists, and exists in the form it does, reasonlessly. It seems at least worth trying to construct a metaphysical theory that reduces some of the arbitrariness of the world. (italics added)

Conclusion

I hope that one conclusion is abundantly clear by now: that the popular image of science as opposed to, or dismissive of, religion no longer holds true. We have seen how the bankruptcy of materialist and mechanistic philosophy has been exposed not only by theologians and religious believers but by hard-nosed scientists who have recognized the need to develop a much fuller understanding of human existence. In doing so, they have demonstrated that contemporary science has far more in common with religious faith than was once thought possible. What is more, neither can do without the other. To quote Einstein, 'Science without religion is lame; religion without science is blind.' Perhaps the time has come to recognize that only when the blind and lame walk together will the journey be made.

PART TWO
The Problem of Suffering

4
God, Suffering and Scepticism

> *Nobody knows what suffering and sacrifice mean – except perhaps the victims.*
>
> Joseph Conrad

The case against the existence of God can be summed up in two words: the Holocaust. If the agnostic really wants to make Christians squirm, he will ask how it is that the kind of God Christians talk about could sit by and let six million Jews be exterminated without lifting a finger. 'Where was God,' he might say, 'when the Nazis were busily gassing men, women and children twenty-four hours a day for three years?' What sort of divine Being would do nothing while scenes like the following were enacted throughout Europe?

> It is estimated that four million people lost their lives in Auschwitz . . . The furnaces in the crematoria became so hot that firebricks cracked, and additional burning pits had to be dug. Once started, the flames were fuelled with the fat that had run off the burning bodies. As at this period it was not considered worth gassing babies and small children, [the SS] would throw them live into the gutters of boiling human fat. (Anton Gill, *The Journey back from Hell*, pp. 26–7)

Burning children in streams of human fat! What kind of God could stand by and allow this to happen? The God of miracles portrayed by the Bible has simply vanished.

Or, rather, he was never there in the first place. Which is more plausible: to believe in a God who does nothing in the face of human evil such as this, or to dismiss the possibility of such a Being's existence? The Christian – or any other religion's – claim that there is a God who acts in the world to bring about good is emphatically negated by the Holocaust. What is more, he appears to have absented himself from human suffering throughout history, not just from the twentieth century. The history of the human race is nothing less than the history of suffering. As the philosopher, Thomas Hobbes, put it three hundred years ago, life is 'nasty, brutish and short.'

Attempted Answers

Of course, it is possible to blunt the force of such criticism by engaging in sophistry and word games. The Church is particularly good at that. Faced with the enormity of suffering over the centuries, it has become a past master at defending the indefensible. Here are some ploys that have been used in the cause of a God whose existence is denied by human experience.

1. The Definition Gambit

According to this, we must distinguish between several different types of suffering. What are sometimes called 'natural evils' are simply part of the way the world is. Earthquakes, typhoons, volcanoes and the like are part of Nature's workings. They can hardly be laid at God's door. He does not directly send catastrophes; they just happen. He cannot be held accountable.

Likewise, we cannot blame God for *human* evil. He cannot be held responsible for the actions of a Ghengis Khan, an Adolf Hitler, a Joseph Stalin or a Pol Pot. The suffering brought about by characters such as these is the outcome of *their* wickedness, not God's.

But although this kind of reasoning may get God off some hooks, it still leaves him impaled on others. Suppose we go back to the issue of natural disasters. It does not help the Christian's case that they are conventionally called 'acts of God'. This implies somehow that they are all his fault. And claiming that they are the outcome of purely natural forces doesn't get us very far either. After all, who created Nature? And who is supposed to be controlling Nature now? Christians cannot have it both ways. Either God is responsible for having made Nature and the way it works or he is not. Either he has the whole world in his hands (as Christians say) or he doesn't. You cannot say, at one and the same time, that God created Nature and keeps it going, yet absolve him of continuing responsibility for its effects. The natural evils argument doesn't work.

Neither does the human wickedness ploy. True, much of the suffering in the world now and throughout history has been caused by human evil. But even so, we're still left with three unanswerable questions:

- Who created human beings in the first place?
- Why couldn't God have made them so that they wouldn't commit evil?
- Why doesn't he intervene to stop the Hitlers of this world?

Once more, we find ourselves left with a God who doesn't seem to have got anything right. He made a mess of human nature to start with and now won't do anything to put it right, or at least prevent its worst excesses. The agnostic could just about stomach a divine Being who stopped the Holocaust coming about in a belated attempt at damage limitation. But Christians can't even point to this kind of God. They're stuck with a Being who is either powerless or sadistic. Not much of a choice, is it?

2. The 'Will of God' Argument

Both Muslims and Christians talk about the will of God/Allah as if this will somehow rescue them from the glaring fact that their theologies are useless in dealing with the brute truths of human existence. To say that the death of millions of innocent men, women and children between 1939 and 1945 (leaving aside the millions who have been tortured and killed before and after) represents the will of God is nothing short of obscene. When this claim is scrutinized, what the apologists are really saying is that God *intended* suffering. Not that he stood by and watched someone else do it, but that he wanted it to happen. This may be unthinkable from the religionist's point of view, but it is the only logical conclusion. The phrase 'will of God' either means this or it means nothing.

3. The Flight into Mystery

More thoughtful religious believers, who have realized the force of the arguments already presented, have attempted to take refuge in an appeal to mystery. 'God is mystery', they claim. 'His ways are beyond our understanding. We must have faith.' This is usually coupled with a statement along the lines that even the most intolerable suffering must have a purpose. The problem is we do not yet know what it could be. If only we trust God and wait, we shall know in the end.

This is pure bunkum. It avoids the harsh questions by rewriting the rules of the game. In one breath we're told that theology is the discipline of thinking and talking about God (in Greek, *theos* means God; *logos* means word) and that human rationality is God-given. Then in the next we find that the greatest obstacle to faith is somehow fenced off from rational discussion and that we must not press reason too far. We are forbidden to inquire rationally into the problem of pain – this will undermine faith. We must simply believe that all will be revealed in the end. Full stop.

This is a neat trick if you can pull it off. And look how many problems it solves. Do we have a belief which looks in danger of collapse when exposed to logic? Then the answer is simple: earmark it 'mystery' and no further discussion becomes necessary. No wonder theology and God have been discredited.

Of course, it is difficult to know whether the flight into mystery is seriously meant. Intellectually, it is completely hollow, as its proponents must know. But still they invoke it. How can religious believers expect a serious hearing when they produce this sort of argument? Indeed, it can scarcely be called an argument since it contains no reasoning at all.

4. The Free Will Defence

This at least has the virtue of presenting an intellectual explanation for suffering. It has undergone several forms since the early church fathers drew it up. But its essence is simple: the existence of evil is the price we pay for possessing freedom. God could have created humanity so that it would never choose to act evilly; but he did not. Not because the task was beyond his reach but because to have programmed us in this way would have removed the possibility of our freely choosing either himself or the good.

The first thing to say about this is that at least the free will defence respects the most important characteristic of being human – our freedom. It was Immanuel Kant, the eighteenth-century Enlightenment philosopher, who showed that true morality cannot exist without the freedom to choose. Being coerced into doing the right thing is hardly a moral act. The people whom Robin Hood forced to give their riches to the poor may have been doing something which brought about good results; but their actions were not the outcome of moral decision. Had they been free to choose, they would have held on to every penny they could! Or, to bring us more up to date, to give £1,000 to charity out of altruism would be regarded as a moral act. To be forced to do so through the taxation system would not. Freedom lies at the heart of morality.

In the same way, for God to have forced human beings always to act morally would amount to a contradiction in terms. The freedom to choose the good can only exist when we are also free to choose the opposite. In short, the possibility of acting evilly is necessary for true morality. If we are not free to choose wrong, then neither are we free to choose right, and morality loses its meaning.

This line of argument has some force. However, when faced with the appalling suffering of the Holocaust we have to ask this: if torturing babies is the price to pay for freedom, is the price worth it? Would it not have been better for God to have avoided creating humanity in the first place than to create us with the capacity for inflicting such terrible atrocities upon the most vulnerable of the species? Is not such a Creator simply callous to the extreme?

Summing up, we find that religionists offer us a God who either

- is powerful enough to stop suffering but does not care; or
- does care but is impotent to act; or
- does not exist.

The first two conceptions of God have only a limited appeal. They certainly do not suffice to address the problem of suffering. That leaves option three. Given the sheer scale of suffering in the world, it offers the only credible conclusion.

The Centrality of the Holocaust

The reader will by now have realized that the driving force behind the agnostic's case has been the *fact* of suffering.

To this, theology supplies only weak answers: God must stay in the dock. It is now time to examine in greater detail the one piece of evidence which for many people remains the decisive charge against him – the Holocaust.

We may begin by noting that Nazism grew directly out of Christian anti-Semitism stretching back over centuries. There is a story told by Adolf Hitler that two Catholic bishops once came to see him to object to his policy towards the Jews. In reply he had only one thing to say: that he couldn't understand their complaint since he was merely finishing what the Church had started.

The history of Christian anti-Semitism in both Catholic and Protestant churches for hundreds of years created the seedbed in which the genocidal policies of the Nazis could flourish. It is ludicrous to suppose that Hitler could have got as far as he did without drawing upon a deeply felt prejudice which was already there. Anyone who doubts this should remember that it was to Luther that he turned for justification when he reissued the great Reformer's diatribe *On the Jews and their Lies* 'without gloss or amendment' as a piece of propaganda designed to show that Nazism had a respectable pedigree. Likewise, in making the Jews wear a yellow badge to identify themselves, Hitler simply adapted what the medieval Catholic Church had done. It was hardly surprising, then, that he could declare himself to be 'acting in accordance with the will of the Almighty Creator. By defending myself against the Jew, I am fighting for the work of the Lord.'

Darrell Fasching, in his book, *Narrative Theology after Auschwitz*, has summed up the issue pointedly:

> The holocaust presents a crisis of faith of cataclysmic proportions for both Jew and Christian. For the Jew the question is whether faith in the God of history is possible after Auschwitz. The victims must wonder how God could allow such an evil to happen. For the Christian,

> the question is just as challenging but for a different reason. It is not just that a great evil has occurred . . . but that the foundations of it were laid by almost two thousand years of Christian anti-Judaism in the form of persecutions, pogroms, and expulsions. (p. 21)

Yet even if all this were *not* true, even if there had been no Christian anti-Semitism and Hitler had still carried out his genocidal ambitions, the theological problems would persist. In short, what was God doing between 1933 and 1945?

Both Jewish and Christian theologians have attempted various responses in defence of God. We have seen some of them. But they are not enough to absolve him. Whatever is said, it cannot begin to address the suffering of the death camps. References to mystery, free will and so on seem insulting when the absolute depths of depravity and agony experienced in the Holocaust are considered. The fancy theorizations of theologians collapse once the doors of the gas chambers are opened. Any attempt to explain the absence of God is drowned out by the screams of six million dead. As Irving Greenberg has put it: 'No statement, theological or otherwise, should be made that would not be credible in the presence of the burning children.'

But what could the religionist say to such children? The answer is: nothing. Talk of freedom, mystery and all the rest remains pathetically hollow. Efforts to get God off the hook prove vacuous. It is better to remain silent.

But that is precisely what theologians and the Church cannot do. They dare not. Their very existence turns upon whether they can offer believable views about life and death, even the slaughter of the innocent. And so we are bombarded with facile statements such as 'Trust in God and you will find meaning and purpose.' Try telling that to the Holocaust victims!

Nonetheless, that is what religionists do. In effect, they

say, 'Never mind the death camps, never mind the genocide, never mind that the consciences of the survivors are tortured daily simply because they *have* survived. Despite everything, God is love. Have faith in Him.'

What could be more appalling? Far better to reject God than to follow the kind of Being that could countenance Auschwitz. In the words of Richard Rubenstein, 'To see any purpose in the death camps, the traditional believer is forced to regard the most demonic, anti-human explosion of all history as a meaningful expression of God's purposes. The idea is simply too obscene for me to accept.'

What, then, is the alternative? Radical theologians, both Jewish and Christian, have arrived at the only possible conclusion: the death of God. This is more than a mere dying of faith *in* God: it is the realization that we can no longer presuppose the existence *of* God other than as the projection of human fantasies onto the cosmos. Faced with the alternative of a bleak and empty universe, it is easy to see why human beings have need of a god-figure who controls their destinies. But if the Holocaust contains any theological lesson at all, it is that no such Being exists. The justification for religious belief which has enabled religion to survive for so long has been that in the end God holds the world in his hands; that whatever humankind may do, he remains faithful.

In a post-Auschwitz world, such belief is no longer credible. Thomas Alitzer expressed the point from a radical Christian standpoint when he said: 'God is not simply hidden from view, nor is he lurking in the depth of our unconscious or on the boundaries of our infinite space . . . the contemporary Christian accepts the death of God as a final and irrevocable event.' And Rubenstein makes a similar point as a Jew: 'We stand in a cold, silent, unfeeling cosmos, unaided by any powerful power beyond our own resources. After Auschwitz, what else can a Jew say about God?'

Far better, then, to accept the impossibility of faith and embrace agnosticism. Freed from the tyranny of forcing oneself to believe in the unbelievable, the individual is liberated to make meaning for herself, not to search for meaning imposed by others, least of all by a God who fails the test of faith. Once we have found this kind of freedom, the universe is ours, and ours alone.

5
Other Voices: Some Alternative Agnosticisms

> *Since history is, first, man's responsibility, we should begin our examination by questioning and discussing man himself.*
>
> Eliezer Berkovits

The arguments of the sceptic in the last chapter represent atheism rather than agnosticism. The agnostic does not rule out the existence of God: he merely defers any final conclusion on the matter. The atheist, on the other hand, is as sure in his conviction that God does not exist as is the religious believer that God does. The case put forward in Chapter 4 is therefore best viewed as a form of 'protest atheism'.

But there are alternatives. Agnosticism comes in many forms, especially on this topic. It remains possible to take seriously the protest of the sceptic while still leaving open the question of God. The Holocaust, for all its horrors, does not require the death of God, merely his refashioning.

In this chapter we shall be considering four views of suffering which leave room for some kind of divine Being, and one which does not (at least in the conventional sense). They each offer an alternative to monotheistic religion on one hand (Christianity, Judaism and Islam) and to atheism on the other. The choice does not have to be between militant scepticism and equally militant religion; there is a middle way.

1. Suffering as an Illusion: Christian Science

According to the nineteenth-century founder of Christian Science, Mary Baker Eddy, what we call evil is an illusion. It has no reality independent of the human mind. 'It is neither person, place, nor thing, but is simply a belief, an illusion of material sense . . . it has no real basis.' From this she goes on to deduce that suffering, too, is illusory: 'The cause of all so-called disease is mental, a mortal fear, a mistaken belief or conviction of the necessity and power of ill-health.' And because suffering springs from the human mind it can be countered by the mind: 'When a sufferer is convinced that there is no reality in his belief in pain . . . how can he suffer longer?'

It is difficult to know what to make of such beliefs. Were it not for the fact that Christian Science has persisted for more than a century (Mary Baker Eddy claimed to have received divine revelation in the 1860s), it would be tempting to write the movement off as unsustainable and cranky. But it continues to grow, and although no official statistics are published, observers estimate its following at about half a million world-wide.

Although it lays great emphasis on the actions of the human mind, Christian Science finds a place for God. He is 'stripping off the disguise' of sin, sickness and death. He is the 'divine Whole, and All, an all-pervading intelligence and love, a divine, infinite principle.' Such language, however, should not be taken to point to an orthodox view of God. In practice, Christian Science is a form of pantheism which identifies God with Nature. And although Mary Baker Eddy denied this was so, it is clear from her writings that when she spoke of 'the Allness of God' she meant that God was not to be thought of as a separate Being from the whole of creation: God and Nature must be seen as one.

Whatever we might think of all this, Christian Science

does offer an alternative to atheism. Moreover, it has the distinct advantage for agnostics of avoiding too rigorous a doctrine of God. Unlike Christianity, Judaism or Islam, it allows us to form whatever picture of God we feel to be most convincing. It offers wide scope for a range of beliefs.

The real problem with Christian Science, though, lies not in its doctrine of God. From an agnostic's point of view the vaguer that is, the better. What is much more questionable is its attempt to wish away suffering as illusory. To continue to hold to such a belief in the light of the history of the twentieth century seems perverse. If we were to apply Greenberg's test, how could Christian Science stand up in the presence of the burning children? What would Mary Baker Eddy have said when presented with the Holocaust? It is these kinds of questions that undermine the credibility of Christian Science as an alternative agnostic approach to suffering.

2. *Two Kinds of Dualism*

If Christian Science identifies God with Nature, dualism does the opposite: it suggests that there are parts of Nature which are opposed to God. Historically, dualism has taken two forms. The first claims that God is not the only power in the universe; that there exists also a malevolent power of equal force which is the source of suffering and evil. This second power was not created by God (as was the devil in traditional Christian theology), but like God has always existed. Consequently the evils we experience in this world are the outcome of this malevolent being at work.

There are two points of significance for us in this. First, suffering will always have a place in human affairs. God and the malevolent being are destined to battle it out for ever. Neither will win a final victory and so the best we can hope for is periodic respites from suffering as God holds the forces of evil temporarily at bay.

Second, this kind of dualism offers an explanation for evil actions and individuals which goes beyond accounting for them in purely natural terms. Hitler and the Holocaust, for example, might be seen as demonic in the sense that behind them lay the cosmic malevolent being opposed to God and the good.

Although highly speculative and couched in crude thought-forms, this account contains some attractions for post-Auschwitz humanity. Standard humanistic explanations, say of Hitler and Nazism, lay emphasis on the historical, social and political forces which gave rise to them. When psychological interpretations are added, we have a picture which is drawn entirely in terms of natural cause and effect.

But to many observers, this seems inadequate. Complex though it may be, a naturalistic interpretation does not seem to go far enough in explaining the depths of absolute evil. When all the sociological, historical, political and psychological explanations have been exhausted, there still remains a dimension to the evil and suffering brought about by the Nazis that defies naturalistic accounts. We find ourselves saying 'Surely there is more to it than this?' Dualism offers a way of interpreting what the 'something more' might be. It invites us to believe in a supernatural force that is more poisoned than we can imagine, a being whose evil is reflected only dimly in a Hitler or a Stalin but whose hand can be seen in their actions. Although cast in crude and outmoded imagery, this kind of dualism has its attractions.

A second version makes suffering the result of inadequacies in the 'stuff' of which creation is made or in the creative skills of the Maker. On this view, God was rather like the potter faced with sub-standard clay. He did the best he could with what was at hand; but in the end the result was imperfect. Alternatively, although the clay was up to scratch, God was not. He lacked the abilities to fashion it without flaws. Either way, suffering was the result.

To us, such an explanation seems fanciful. But just as the first version of dualism found favour in the classical world, so the second was advanced in all seriousness by the nineteenth-century philosopher, John Stuart Mill. Speaking of 'the obstacles which partially thwart what seem the purposes of the Creator', he ascribes 'the limitations of his power' either to 'the qualities of the material – the substance and forces of which the universe is composed' or to the inadequacies of divine abilities: 'the Creator did not know how to do it; creative skill, wonderful as it is, was not sufficiently perfect to accomplish his purposes more thoroughly.'

Once again, we need to note that however strange either dualism may appear at the end of the twentieth century, both versions continue to have their adherents. This is especially true of the first where we do not have to look to so-called 'primitive' societies to see it at work: we have only to observe Western culture's curiosity about the supernatural and the occult. The writings of best-seller Stephen King testify amply to the credibility of dualistic ideas. Even for supposedly scientific societies, there are some kinds of suffering and evil that are simply too profound to be explained in purely human terms.

3. Deism and the Cosmic Machine Minder

Deism is the belief that although there exists a supreme Being whom we call God, such a Being is impersonal, distant and detached. He may have created the universe but he plays no part in its continuance. To use an image popular in the eighteenth century, God can be likened to a watchmaker who, having created a cosmic mechanism, left it to run of its own accord, in conformity with the laws of nature he had established. As William Paley, a theologian of the time, put it: 'every indication, every manifestation of design, which existed in the watch, exists in the works of nature.'

There are two possible – though contradictory – implications of such a view for the problem of suffering. On one hand, it might be viewed as a failure in the machinery, a breakdown in the smooth functioning of the natural order. (Let us call this Deism A.) The malfunction could be due to a design fault (God got it wrong) or to the inadequacy of the materials he used (back to dualism again?). Whatever the reason, the result is the same: suffering is a blight.

But there is an alternative possibility which assigns a rather more positive role to suffering. (We can call this Deism B.) On this account, suffering is a necessary part of the machine's functioning, indicating not breakdown but development. At this point we see the theory of evolution coming into its own. Prior to Darwin, apologists for deism had no scientifically credible way of accounting for suffering. They could not show persuasively how it might actually contribute to the working of the machine.

Darwin, however, changed all that. Much of the apparently useless misery we see in the world has a purpose after all. It can be put down to the inevitability of the evolutionary process. Survival of the fittest requires that suffering take place; it is the price to be paid for the growth and development of the myriad life forms that exist. It is a necessary part of the way the natural order progresses, the way the machine works to maximize the outcome.

On this view, therefore, it becomes possible to regard evolution not as destructive and wasteful but as constructive and purposeful. True, it is a great destroyer – think of the millions of animal and human lives destroyed by the process. But the end product is profoundly constructive. In the words of the Oxford biologist, Richard Dawkins, natural selection is not only a 'negative force, capable of weeding out freaks and failures' but also 'capable of building up complexity, beauty and efficiency of design.'

However, Dawkins is an atheist rather than an agnostic. He believes that Paley's argument is false because blind evolution achieves the same outcome as deistic design: 'the living results of natural selection overwhelmingly impress us with the *illusion* of design and planning.' We might think that the world has been deliberately planned to be as orderly and elegant as a watch but this is mere appearance. Evolution has achieved the trick without a deity. The God hypothesis is rendered unnecessary.

We do not have to go all the way with Dawkins' atheism to see that evolution has a purpose in the great scheme of things. It would be possible to hold to an agnostic position while at the same time thinking of evolution as God's chosen means of bringing order out of chaos, the outstanding example of divinely established natural laws. Deism and Darwin go well together: the absentee God working through the impersonal mechanism of natural selection.

This is all very neat. However, it does nothing to solve the *moral* problem of suffering. It fails the Greenberg test completely and utterly. Indeed, we have only to recall that at the heart of the Nazi creed lay a belief in social Darwinianism – the view that society itself was composed of individuals engaged in a struggle for existence in which only the fittest survived. In Hitler's words, 'He who wants to live must fight, and he who does not want to fight in this world where eternal struggle is the law of life has no right to exist.'

The translation of this principle into a political programme issued in the death of millions of innocent people. Far from offering a solution to the problem of suffering, evolution merely provided a warped justification for inflicting it.

But even if social Darwinism had never been thought of, we would still be left with a massive problem: why did the deistic God have to build a machine that was driven by such an arbitrary, wasteful and cruel mechanism? Surely he could have done it another way? This version of agnosticism gets us no further than traditional monotheistic religion. It ends up impaling itself on the same hook.

So where does that leave us? Do we have to dump deism altogether? Possibly not. It can still be salvaged for the agnostic; but only by reverting to Deism A: the belief that the divinely created cosmic machine has somehow gone wrong. This avoids the arbitrariness of Deism B, though it fails to offer any credible explanation for the place of evolution. Is it a brute fact, a mystery or a breakdown? It seems whichever way we turn, deism is beset with insoluble problems; the Creator in Deism A is too weak to have created a properly functioning machine in the first place, too absent to keep it running in the event of breakdown, or too heartless to bother. The Divine Being of Deism B has devised an efficient mechanism in the shape of evolution but lacks compassion. Either way, deism seems not to contain the answer.

4. New Age Agnostics?

So what is left? None of the options for agnostics we have considered so far has proved any more successful than full-blown religious faith on the one hand and outright atheism on the other. In this final section we shall consider one further possibility. Its technical name is monism but it is perhaps best recognized under the guise of New Age philosophy.

Monism has a long history. It lies at the opposite pole to dualism. Instead of two supernatural Beings battling it out, in monism there is no supernatural Being at all. Everything is knit together in a single harmonious unity. There is no separate God: he is identical with the whole of creation. As Joyce Watson puts it:

> Fundamental to the whole concept of the New Age is Monism, the belief that All is one. God is understood to be cosmic energy, universal energy, or the life force, flowing in and through everything. All is God and there is no distinction between the Creator and creation. The aim of every person seriously involved in the New Age is to connect with the life force. They believe that humanity is on the threshold of a major evolutionary leap into a higher spiritual state, in which a person realises that he or she is divine, totally at one with God. (*A Guide to the New Age for Confused Christians*, p. 5)

Shirley Maclaine is perhaps one of the best known exponents of such a view. She writes: 'I know that I exist, therefore I AM. I know the God-source exists. Therefore IT IS. Since I am part of that force, then I AM that I AM.'

This equation of humanity with God reflects the monism of New Age thinking and is echoed by the physicist-cum-mystic, Fritjof Capra, who points out that the ultimate state of consciousness is one 'in which all boundaries and dualisms have been transcended and all individuality dissolves into universal, undifferentiated oneness.' Similarly, the concept of God suggested by Jane Roberts links both monism and pantheism:

> He is not one individual, but an energy gestalt . . . a psychic pyramid of interrelated, ever-expanding consciousness that creates, simultaneously and instantly, universes and individuals that are given – through the gift of personal perspective – duration, psychic comprehension, intelligence, and eternal validity . . . Its energy is so unbelievable that it does indeed form all universes;

> and because its energy is within and behind all universes, systems and fields, it is indeed aware of each sparrow that falls, for it is each sparrow that falls.

It is on the basis of this kind of thinking that Benjamin Creme comments: 'In a sense there is no such thing as God, God does not exist. And in another sense, there is nothing else but God – only God exists . . . All is God. And because all is God, there is no God.'

What are we to make of such rhetoric? Its descent into vague, quasi-mystical jargon almost defies analysis. However, what is clear is that the combination of monism and pantheism we find in New Age thinking makes it extraordinarily difficult to see how it could generate an adequate explanation for suffering.

It is perhaps no coincidence that such a world-view has grown up in the comfortable, materialistic West. For it offers just the right cocktail of optimistic, unconventional, non-institutional religion that would appeal to people disillusioned with science and traditional religion alike. However, it runs into one massive problem: what to do with the existence of suffering? It disrupts the harmony of the whole.

In practice, the only way of fitting suffering into the scheme is either to deny its reality (as in Christian Science) or to see it as an unavoidable part of the way the universe is. Since there is no God in the conventional sense, he cannot be blamed for having created a flawed universe or for allowing suffering to enter in.

These are mere word games, however. Redefining suffering or viewing it as an illusion that could be overcome by altering our way of looking at it does not remove its force. It is still there. People fall ill, animals are killed, babies still burn. New Age thinking does nothing to change these facts or to remove their destructiveness.

It is hard to see, then, how monism – even in its up-to-date New Age version – can solve the problem of suffering, despite its abandonment of traditional ideas of God. Certainly it remains an option for the agnostic who wants to keep the door open for God in some sense. But it offers a solution which presents only false promises. This option turns out to be no better than any other.

Conclusion

It looks as if we are back to a stark choice: protest atheism or traditional religion. These seem to be the only viable alternatives, given the enormity of the problem of suffering. The four possibilities outlined in this chapter are no more credible (and in some cases a lot less so) than the two original positions. If the agnostic were to follow Christian Science, dualism, deism or New Age philosophies, he would either end up with a God who was too feeble to act or too heartless to bother. Or he would be forced to deny the existence of a problem at all. None of these is satisfactory. As we shall see, it would be better to be an atheist or a believer.

6
God in the Wasteland

A God who cannot suffer is poorer than any man.
Jürgen Moltmann

If the only choice on offer is between atheism and faith, why choose faith? This is the challenge thrown at the religionist every time she watches the TV news. And it has been used to considerable effect. When faced with suffering, the believer invariably goes on the defensive.

But why should this be the case? We can turn the challenge on its head: why choose atheism – or its pale imitation, agnosticism? The existence of pain and evil is as much a threat to atheism as it is to faith. In this chapter we shall be exploring why this is so and why, in the end, atheism provides an even less credible answer than religious belief.

More positively, we shall also see how Christian theology enables us to have faith in a God who is neither powerless nor distant; a God who shares in humanity's suffering yet who has overcome it. The stereotypes of earlier chapters simply do not fit this kind of God.

Why Atheism Will Not Do

When faced with the Holocaust, atheism leads to an even more unpalatable conclusion than does religion. For if there is no God, no reality other than the life we experience here and now, then the past, present and future are truly bleak. It is one thing to rail against God for having supposedly stood back while human beings and nature colluded in their infliction of death and destruction. But it is quite another to remove God from the scene altogether. Only then is the true barrenness of atheism fully revealed. With no God to hold accountable, everything collapses into meaninglessness.

This is the inevitable logic of atheism. If the only reality that exists is the material universe we see around us, it follows that there is no ultimate meaning or truth – merely a collection of competing claims to such. The Holocaust and all the other atrocities in history are just events without meaning. They are sick jokes.

But can we live with the implications of this? History suggests not. Human beings need to give meaning to their lives and to make sense of their experiences. Religious faith once gave such meaning. When faith is jettisoned, we find ourselves left with a clockwork universe devoid of ultimate truth or purpose. It is just *there*. The only way we can discover meaning is to invent it.

But this leads into all sorts of quagmires. How are we to distinguish between rival claims to have found the 'true meaning of existence'? After all, on the atheist account, we are unable to appeal to God or some supernatural truth. They do not exist. All we can do is to assign interpretations to events and construct meanings as we see fit. It is all down to us. But who is to say which interpretations are true? Atheism offers no way ahead, only a blind alley. Eliezer Berkovits, a post-Holocaust Jewish theologian, makes the point well. According to atheism, he concludes,

> The only meanings, the only values, are those created by man. There is nothing beyond this existence, beyond this ethical indifference of the cosmos. There is no possibility for any reference to the transcendental for

> values and standards. Life is altogether man's responsibility, his choice and his decision; it is his fight against meaningless fate. The meaning that man alone can create is the only justification for a meaningless universe.

The problem with this approach, though, is that it offers no way of deciding who has got the 'correct' interpretation. All we find is a plethora of competing views without any coherent criteria to choose between them. Here is Berkovits again: 'If there is no possibility for a transcendental value-reference, if existence as such is fundamentally meaningless and man alone is the creator of values, who is to determine what the values are going to be, or what the man-made meaning is to be? Man of course. But which man?'

The Holocaust provides us with a case in point. To modern Western societies, it was an act of unambiguous genocidal evil. Yet to the Nazi, and to today's neo-Nazis, it was a noble cause, the extermination of the Jews a moral duty, a cleansing of the world from their pollution. To quote Heinrich Himmler, 'This is a glorious page in our history, never before, never again to be written.'

So how are we to decide who is right? On the basis of atheism, there is no rational way. Our choices must be arbitrary, based on personal, subjective and cultural factors. We cannot appeal to any set of transcendent values, for everything is but an aspect of the material universe. There is no God to tell us what is right and wrong. We just have to decide for ourselves. Which is exactly what Hitler did. If atheism is true, says Berkovits,

> Why should one not be able to opt, in the full honesty of one's self-made truth, for the idea of a master race as the supreme man-created value? It is true that far greater human suffering is likely to be found in a world in which the master race idea constitutes the meaning of life, but this is the complaint of those who suffer.

> The infliction of suffering may well be reconciled – as indeed it has often been – with the man-made values and meanings of the persecutors. Some like to side with the persecuted; others enjoy cherry pie, while others again find meaning in an otherwise absurd universe by feeding the crematoria with human bodies. In a universe in which all values are based on human choice and decision anything may become such a value. (*Faith after the Holocaust*, p. 72)

At this point, the atheist might object that there is such a thing as natural morality; that we can instinctively know right from wrong because they are built into the natural order. Natural justice demands that we condemn the Holocaust as absolutely wrong. This may sound fine but it is illogical: how can nature – which is by definition neutral – generate values? The natural order is simply a collection of matter; it cannot give us rights and wrongs. Like the rest of the universe, it is a brute fact.

We are back, then, to viewing meaning as something imposed upon reality by the human mind and all the circularity that this view entails. Atheism simply cannot offer a coherent account of why we should regard some things as right and others as wrong; unless, of course, we invoke a moral imperative that we can show takes precedence over all others – say, justice, or love? But once we do this, we have to ask, 'Why choose these values rather than, say, survival of the fittest?' Indeed, there seems a much stronger case for invoking this than love or justice precisely because survival is the most fundamental imperative of all.

But look where such a move gets us. As soon as we appeal to survival, we quickly find ourselves asking, 'Survival for whom?' The Nazis were convinced they knew, of course: the master race. In the light of the history of the twentieth century, is a survival ethic really enough?

This is not the only problem for atheism, however. What about the Greenberg test? What has atheism to say to the burning children? That the Holocaust was just 'one of those things'? That it was merely an unfortunate fact of history? That it was a meaningless event in a meaningless cosmos? None of these is acceptable. Atheism is the most cruel hypothesis of all. For it says that in the end, injustice cannot be righted, suffering cannot be redeemed, evil triumphs after all. There is nothing more the atheist can say to the victims of Auschwitz.

Hence protest atheism turns out to be a dead end. It rages with all the indignation Western liberalism can muster – but against what? Not against God since he doesn't exist. Against the impersonal cosmos then? Or social Darwinism? Whichever it is, such rage is morally empty. It does no more than allow us to vent our anger. Hence on the Greenberg test, we can offer no meaning to the victims which does not insult them. We are left with a cold, bleak, empty universe. Is this truly to be preferred to faith in a creator God who, despite the existence of suffering, is at work to bring good out of evil?

The implications of all this are enormous. We can scarcely grasp them because we live sheltered and comfortable lives. We have built meaning for ourselves through our jobs, our families, our goals. But if we were to remove these, what would we be left with? Nothing but meaninglessness. In the words of Albert Camus, we would be stuck with no more than 'that hopeless encounter between human questioning and the silence of the universe'. Little wonder that Bertrand Russell wrote: 'Only on the firm foundation of unyielding despair can the soul's habitation be safely built.' (Russell could afford to say this. He was writing from the groves of academe rather than from the gas chambers of the Holocaust.)

So atheism fails on three counts:

1. it offers insufficient and incoherent grounds for making moral choices;
2. it leaves us surrounded by meaninglessness; and
3. it does nothing to address the problem of suffering.

Despite this, of course, there are still many who would call themselves atheists. But in doing so they merely have rejected one kind of faith for another. To hold that atheism is true is every bit as much an act of faith as that practised by the most religious of people. We should not blind ourselves to this.

What, then, is the alternative? If atheism is no better than religion, where do we go from here?

Although the focus of our discussion will be upon how Christian theology might offer us a way forward, it is worth remembering in passing that post-Holocaust Judaism has also had to grapple with these questions. And although one response has been to abandon Jewish faith altogether, such a reaction has not been the dominant one.

A Christian Alternative

It is now time to return to the original problem of suffering as we identified it in Chapter 4:

- If God is all powerful and all loving, as Christians claim, then why does he not intervene to prevent evil and suffering? Since they so obviously exist, he must be either impotent or heartless.

To set the question up in this way, however, begs one overriding issue: what kind of interventionist God do we want? For, make no mistake, to ask for God to step in constantly to prevent human or natural causes of suffering would be to ask for a puppet-master, nothing less. Every time you or I or someone else did something that would lead to suffering, God would have to intervene either to stop us from acting in the first place or to mitigate the consequences of our actions.

This is impossible to imagine for a number of reasons. First, there is the issue of what this would mean in practice. God would have to control both our deeds and our thoughts. Every part of our lives would have to be manipulated so as to prevent suffering from appearing. Even our smallest thoughts would be subject to divine control.

Neither could God stop at thoughts and acts which would *directly* bring about suffering. He would also have to take action *indirectly*. For there are many things we do that are simply links in a causal chain of which we have only limited awareness. Suppose, for example, that I unintentionally oversleep one morning because the alarm clock breaks down. I rush out of the house in a desperate attempt not to be late for work. But as I drive out, I fail to look to the right as a cyclist is coming along. Wham! I hit her. She is severely injured, as a result of which she is permanently disabled. She loses her job. Her family suffers.

Now here is a clear case of unintentional suffering. What would God have to do in order to prevent it happening? At what point along the chain of cause and effect would we want him to intervene? And how, exactly?

The possibilities are legion: he could wake me up earlier by natural means. He could cause the phone to ring which would mean that I left the house five minutes later. He could cause a puncture in the cyclist's tyre so as to slow her up before reaching my gate. And so on . . .

But look at what we are asking: no less than for God to pull the strings not just in my life but in the lives of all the others in this example – the cyclist, the person who rings me up, the alarm clock manufacturer. Do we really want this kind of God? He would never leave us alone. Our lives would be completely regulated.

Second, we are faced with the problem of the natural order. Volcanoes, earthquakes and famines are all part of the world as we know it. To prevent all suffering that derived from them would require God unceasingly to change the regularities which govern nature and on which we depend. The laws of physics would be rendered meaningless since we could count on nothing to happen as we might predict. And given that we now know by means of chaos theory that small actions in one part of the world can bring about disproportionate and unforeseen effects elsewhere, we should have to expect God to intervene throughout the whole of the system at all times. Predictability would drop to zero and science as we know it would collapse. Indeed, we should be reduced to such a state of physical, social and psychological instability that life would fall apart, paradoxically bringing even more suffering in its train.

Third, what would happen to morality? We noted earlier that for human beings to act genuinely morally, they need to be free to choose. But this is exactly what we would be denying if we expected God to block our actions or relieve us of their consequences at every twist and turn. And since moral freedom is what makes human beings distinctive out of the whole of creation, it is hard to see how this could be reconciled with a God whose actions would be aimed at frustrating such freedom. For God to shield us from ourselves would be to ask for Big Brother with a vengeance.

So what are we left with? In part, the well-trodden free will defence, at least in respect of human actions. But we have also invoked what John Polkinghorne, former Professor of Mathematical Physics at Cambridge, has called the 'free process defence'. In other words, for human beings to be allowed to flourish, creation must in some sense also be free to behave in accordance with its nature. In the case of earthquakes, for example, this means allowing tectonic plates to slip about as they will, unless (and this is a very big 'unless') human beings, exercising *their* freedom, were to find a way to stop this from happening. As Polkinghorne comments in his book, *Serious Talk*,

> The God of love will endow his creation with an appropriate measure of freedom. God cannot exert the unrelaxing grip of a cosmic tyrant; rather, God must allow the other to be truly itself . . . creation involves God in a voluntary self-limitation as he graciously allows something other than himself to have a genuine life of its own. (p. 52)

But does such an argument not take us back to views akin to deism? This is where the distinctive claims of Christian belief have something crucial to teach us.

The God Who Suffers

The God of the Bible and of Christian theology is not the God of the deists for the simple reason that he cares. And what is more, his care is shown in the central claim of Christian faith: that Jesus Christ was crucified and three days later rose from the dead. This is nothing short of astounding. What is being said is that the death of a young Nazarene two millennia ago, followed by his return to life, somehow address the problem of suffering down the ages; that the cross and the empty tomb have a relevance even to Auschwitz.

We shall see in the final section of this book more of the meaning and significance of Jesus of Nazareth. But for the time being, we need to take hold of three points.

First, in the death of Christ, God was entering into the suffering of humankind without reservation. This is not easy to grasp, for we are so used to thinking of God in deistic terms. But the Christian gospel is clear: God understands our suffering because he has experienced it. He is not the distant supreme Being who knows nothing of what his creatures undergo; he has felt the pain of the world through the pain of his Son. As Professor Richard Bauckham has put it: 'The cross does not absolve God of responsibility for suffering. Rather it shows that the one who bears overall responsibility for this suffering world is on the side of those who suffer to the extent of sharing their pain and adopting their cause.'

Second, if God himself has suffered alongside humanity – and especially alongside the innocent, as the crucifixion of his innocent Son shows – it becomes possible to find meaning even within such horrors as the death camps. Suffering does not have to be seen as a sick joke. If God suffers with us, he can be discovered by us. His solidarity with the godforsaken becomes the means by which those same godforsaken can find love. Bauckham cites the German theologian Jürgen Moltmann to this effect: 'The suffering of abandonment is overcome by the suffering of love, which is not afraid of what is sick and ugly, but accepts it and takes it to itself in order to heal it.'

But how is healing to be accomplished? This brings us to our third point. Not by the waving of a cosmic wand or the easy slogans of organized religion, to be sure. Rather, the embracing of suffering by Jesus (and through him by his Father) is completed only by the resurrection of the selfsame Son. By this once-for-all act, God was demonstrating that suffering and evil could not have the last word. Had the life of Jesus ended with the crucifixion, we would still be left with a powerless God. But through the resurrection, the power of God for the healing of the world and the overcoming of suffering was revealed for all time. We shall see more of this in Chapter 9.

Conclusion

We have seen how the Christian might respond to the atheist's and agnostic's charge that suffering denies the possibility of God. In doing so, we have observed that those who level this charge are caught in no lesser trap. Their arguments against religion simply throw all the protest back upon atheism and agnosticism – for which they in turn have no answer.

But most of all, we have seen that Christian belief has something much more robust to proclaim, namely the suffering love of Jesus' crucifixion and the power of his resurrection. A piece entitled *The Long Silence* makes the point with force:

> At the end of time, billions of people were scattered on a great plain before God's throne. Most shrank back from the brilliant light before them. But some groups near the front talked heatedly – not with cringing shame but with belligerence. 'Can God judge us?'
>
> 'How can he know about suffering?' snapped a pert young brunette. She ripped open a sleeve to reveal a tattooed number from a Nazi concentration camp. 'We endured terror . . . beating . . . torture . . . death!'
>
> In another group a black man lowered his collar. 'What about this?' he demanded, showing an ugly rope burn. 'Lynched for no crime but being black!'
>
> In another crowd, a pregnant schoolgirl with sullen eyes. 'Why should I suffer?' she murmured. 'It wasn't my fault.'
>
> Far out across the plain were hundreds of such groups. Each had a complaint against God for the evil and suffering he had permitted in his world. How lucky God was to live in heaven where all was sweetness and light, where there was no weeping or fear, no hunger or hatred. What did God know of all that men had been enforced to endure in this world? For God leads a pretty sheltered life, they said.
>
> So each of these groups sent forth their leader, chosen because he had suffered the most. A Jew, a black, a person from Hiroshima, a horribly disabled arthritic, a

thalidomide child. In the centre of the plain they consulted with each other.

At last they were ready to present their case. It was rather clever. Before God could be qualified to be their judge, he must endure what they had endured. Their verdict was that God should be sentenced to live on earth – as a man! Let him be born a Jew. Let the legitimacy of his birth be doubted. Give him a work so difficult that even his family will think him out of his mind when he tries to do it. Let him be betrayed by his closest friends. Let him face false charges, be tried by a prejudiced jury and convicted by a cowardly judge. Let him be tortured. At last, let him see what it means to be terribly alone. Then let him die in agony. Let him die so that there can be no doubt he died. Let there be a whole host of witnesses to verify it.

As each leader announced the portion of his sentence, loud murmurs of approval went up from the throng of people assembled. When the last had finished pronouncing sentence there was a long silence. No one uttered another word. No one moved. For suddenly all knew that God had already served his sentence.

PART THREE
Jesus Christ

7
Man, Myth or God?

History is bunk.
Henry Ford

Scratch the surface of Christianity and you will soon find Jesus Christ. Without him, it would be nothing. Besides being its founder, he is also its central enigma. Yet what can we say about him with any degree of assurance?

Christians, of course, answer 'quite a lot'. They remain convinced that the records we have of his life – the four Gospels – are biographical and that they should be seen as historical accounts containing factual information about this man from Nazareth. Never mind that they are fantastical in what they recount; as far as the Christian Church is concerned, they belong to the realm of historical fact.

The problem with this is that for any unbiased observer, the Gospels are completely unlike history as we know it. No modern scientific historian could possibly accept them merely on their own say-so. She would need corroborating evidence to back up the bizarre statements made not only *by* Jesus but *about* him. What is more, given the magnitude of the issues at stake – the resurrection of dead people, for example – she would be duty-bound to err on the side of doubt until the evidence conclusively proved otherwise. Her integrity as an historian would demand no less.

In this chapter, it will be argued that the claims of

Christianity about its founder are so extraordinary and unverifiable that they must be regarded as no more than expressions of the inner psychological states of those who put them forward. People who talk about Jesus Christ as some kind of God–man are, literally, speaking non-sense. They may be saying something about their own frame of mind or faith orientation; but they are saying nothing that will pass the test of objectivity. At best, Christians are well-meaning wishful thinkers, at worst, they are deluded. What they are *not* is bearers of provable historical truth.

The implication of all this is that we must remain agnostic about the founder of the Christian religion. There is no point in denying that he ever existed (as some Marxists once did). That there was a man whom we call Jesus of Nazareth who wandered through Palestine about two thousand years ago need not be disputed. That he was a wise teacher who identified with the poor raises no problems. That he was executed, at least in part for political reasons, can be conceded. But beyond that – who knows? The claim that he performed miracles, was raised from the dead, ascended into heaven as the Son of God and somehow is with us today is of a wholly different order and must be *dis*believed until the burden of proof suggests otherwise.

1. The Gospels and History

Imagine this: a man named Joshua is executed by firing squad for crimes against the state. Yet, apart from the bare record of his execution contained in official files, there is no other evidence of the events in his life until forty years later when a written account begins to circulate, detailing the things he did during his last three years and telling the world what a wonderful man he had been. And, as if a gap of four decades were not enough to cast doubt upon the veracity of this account, it turns out to have been written by his closest friend, seeking to win converts to the cause Joshua had espoused.

Faced with such a situation, what would we think? To be sure, we would immediately be suspicious. A number of questions would come to mind. Why did it take so long before the account was produced? How could we possibly trust the memories of witnesses to events which were supposed to have taken place forty years previously? And what were the motives of the friend in circulating this 'history'?

In short, we would be doubtful as to the authenticity and truthfulness of the stories. We would want to know how they had been compiled, the reliability of the witnesses, what axes they had to grind, and so on. To accept the account uncritically would amount to intellectual dereliction of duty.

Yet this is exactly what Christians have done with their Gospels for twenty centuries. They have placed absolute trust in documents which even at the earliest reckoning were not written until thirty-five to forty years after the death of their central character; and in one case – the Gospel of John – not until seventy years or more.

But carry our imaginary scenario further. Suppose that not just one account of Joshua's life had been produced, but four. Much better we might think. More evidence to substantiate the first. However, upon closer examination, it turns out that there are serious contradictions between the accounts. Two of the four attribute a saying to Joshua which they claim he made in Birmingham city centre in September during the first year of his public life. The others claim he said it three years later in January in Hull. In fact, the more the four accounts are studied, the greater the confusion becomes. Dates, places and speeches are all muddled up. There are glaring inconsistencies throughout. What are we to make of it all?

Certainly, if we had our wits about us, we would doubt

whether the four documents were accurate. We would want to investigate much more thoroughly before concluding any or all of the accounts to be trustworthy. We might, in the end, suspend judgement indefinitely or even discount the stories altogether. At the very least, we would hold back from simply accepting everything they said.

But this is precisely what Christianity has failed to do. It has taken the Gospels at face value. It has accepted them as factually true without question. And when contradictions and inconsistencies have been pointed out, it has ignored them or tried to explain them away. The most rational conclusion must be that the so-called 'biographies' of Jesus Christ amount to little more than a set of fictions.

How and why this has arisen is easy to surmise. The first Christians were desperate to win adherents to a faith to which they had dedicated their lives. It was but a small step to turn the sage-cum-martyr from Nazareth into the divine man. Miracle stories, culminating in the supreme miracle story of the resurrection, were concocted to portray Jesus as superhuman. The Gospel writers, determined to present their central figure as the saviour of the world, constructed Christ in the image of their choosing. The Jesus of the New Testament is much more a reflection of the Gospel writers' projections than of the real man from Galilee.

2. *In Whose Image?*

It is bad enough that the Gospel writers constructed their own Jesus. When we turn to the ways in which he has been portrayed by the Church down the ages, we find an even more confusing kaleidoscope of images. Each generation has projected its own wishful thinking on to the Jesus of the Gospels. In turn he has been the apocalyptic visionary, the political revolutionary, the black Messiah, the Western liberal, the founder of a secret society and the superstar.

Each Christmas, millions flock to adore the babe in the manger and in doing so merely reflect the sentimentality of our age. The baby Jesus, so beloved of those who never attend worship at any other time, is actually no more than the product of late-twentieth-century Western obsession with children.

Interestingly, it was a theologian who first pointed this out. Albert Schweitzer, at the turn of the century, noted that every attempt to discover Jesus objectively had ended up a failure. Invariably, those who went in search of the historical Jesus did not so much find him as find a reflection of themselves. In the history of scholarship, comments Schweitzer, 'each individual created [Jesus] in accordance with his own character.'

When we apply this line of reasoning to the Bible, we quickly realize that we are faced with a twofold difficulty. In the first place, we are not given plain *facts* about Jesus but rather *interpretations*. The Gospel writers present us with myriad pictures full of their own biases and preconceptions. Their versions of Jesus owe more to their own contexts than to what he actually might have said or done. Added to this, in the second place, we are faced with the same process at work within the development of the Church. For two millennia, theologians and clerical politicians have been busy devising Jesus Christ to meet their own agendas. In the light of all this, the only reasonable stance must be that of the agnostic: the most we can say is that Jesus of Nazareth lived and died. Everything else is mere conjecture.

3. Miracles

To the modern person, the New Testament stories of Jesus are much closer to fairy tales than to history. The thought that Jesus could heal a blind man by putting spit-soaked mud on his eyes or drive out demons from a lunatic into a herd of pigs is an offence against reason. These things simply do not happen. Some people might believe they do, but this is what psychologists call wish projection. If anything resembling the miracle stories of the Gospels did take place, they can easily be explained either as embellishments by the writers intent on proving Jesus to be divine or as incidents now capable of rational interpretation. Whichever we choose, we don't need to resort to superstition to explain what happened (if anything). Laws of natural cause and effect will do; superhero-type legends will not.

The Scottish philosopher of the Enlightenment, David Hume, perhaps best expressed the sceptic's case. It remains a case worth examining; for its hard-headed logic is far better suited to the issue at stake than the woolly, unthinking faith which suffuses the utterances of religionists. Interestingly, Hume's central argument has stood the test of time and is still employed by sceptical philosophers today.

Hume's argument begins from a thoroughly modern starting point. Miraculous claims, he says, must be assessed according to the strength of the evidence offered to support them; they must be 'proportioned' to such evidence. This is so obvious that it seems unnecessary to state. Yet religious believers invariably ignore it. They prefer to believe on the basis of the flimsiest of evidence instead. They are prepared to accept testimony that would be torn apart in a court of law as self-delusion, deception or explicable in other ways. When a latter-day healer stands on stage (for theatre is what we are talking about) to proclaim that God has restored Jimmy or Jane to health after the prayer of the faithful – especially *his* prayer, suitably accompanied by the sound of money dropping into the collection plate – he can invariably be shown to be a fool or a knave. This is relatively easy to prove.

But when we look at the biblical accounts, how much more frail is the evidence. Why? Simply because it all comes from sources who had a point to prove anyway. After all, if you were seeking to demonstrate the force of a new religious movement, wouldn't you want to drum up a few miracles?

Here, Hume's argument takes a further turn. Even if the New Testament witnesses were sincere in their belief that Jesus did go around performing miraculous deeds, this doesn't prove they were accurate. To begin with, they might simply have been mistaken in what they saw. We all know how prone human beings are to seeing what they want to see. Second, in judging the value of witness statements, whether as historians or detectives, we invariably place greater value on evidence that corresponds with our own view of the world than on evidence which lies beyond our experience or comprehension. And since very few of us have directly experienced incontrovertible 'miracles', it follows that we must remain sceptical of the claims of those who think they have.

If, for example, a woman came to us claiming to have been abducted by aliens, impregnated by their leader, and subsequently returned to earth, we would rightly treat her story with a high degree of suspicion. In fact, we would probably laugh her out of court or think her insane. Not because we necessarily thought she was deliberately lying (she may have been telling the truth as she saw it), but because we know that the likelihood of such a thing's happening is very remote indeed. And without corroborating evidence the proper response would be to treat her claim with disbelief. Only if a significant number of other people who were not disturbed turned up as witnesses to similar experiences would we begin to take notice. Likewise, we have a duty to suspend belief when confronted with biblical miracles.

To this, Hume adds three further arguments. First, since experience shows that humans are incurably prone to gossip and exaggeration, we have to suppose that this is what happened in biblical times. Without access to the claimants, we cannot vouch for what they say. The most we can do is to remain agnostic.

Second, miracle claims tend to arise in cultures which are pre-scientific and non-rational. Where science has advanced, so miracle claims have diminished. As people have come to understand natural processes, they have been increasingly able to explain phenomena without recourse to the supernatural. And even where no scientific explanation is immediately available, it doesn't follow that there never will be one. The history of science shows that what may be little understood in one era or society will be fully explicable in another. The fact that we no longer believe that sicknesses are the result of ill humours in the blood which require purging and leeching is an obvious case. There are many more.

Third, since miracle claims are found in all kinds of religions and are attributed to competing divinities, they must be reckoned to cancel one another out. This perhaps is the most whimsical of Hume's arguments, though it does have an element of truth. After all, if religions with contradictory belief systems all claim that *their* miracles prove the existence of *their* god and the veracity of *their* beliefs, they cannot all be true. And since it is impossible to judge between them, far better to disregard them all. There must be an equality of scepticism.

Hume's conclusion, then, is one which we must embrace: the claim to miracles is illusory. They prove nothing and can certainly not provide foundations for belief. The only logical position to take is that of the sceptical agnostic.

4. The Resurrection

Dig through to the core of Christianity and you will discover the resurrection of Jesus Christ. Strip it out, and what's left? Not much more than some moral exhortations and a philosophy of love. There is nothing extraordinary about these. Yet if Hume's reasoning requires us to be sceptical about lesser miracles, how much more so when faced with the claim that God raised Jesus from death? Indeed it is significant that Hume used the example of the resurrection to illustrate his thesis. For of all miracles it remains the most breathtaking. The claim to have conquered death is surely the most amazing any religion could make.

Belief in the resurrection, however, is open to scepticism on three counts:

1. the improbability of miracles (Hume's argument above);
2. the bias of the Gospel writers; and
3. the availability of alternative explanations for what happened to Jesus' body after death.

We shall explore the improbability argument in the remainder of this chapter. Points 2 and 3 will be discussed in Chapters 8 and 9.

The Improbability of Miracles

If Hume's scepticism about miracles as such is valid, then it follows that the same kind of reasoning which ruled out 'ordinary' miracles applies equally to the resurrection. To see how this is so, we shall summarize Hume's argument step by step, followed by his own words:

- Step 1 Belief must be proportional to the evidence. Since the assured evidence for the resurrection is highly dubious, we should discount the probability of its having happened. The miracle of resurrection is recorded only rarely in the New Testament. Over and against these statistically insignificant instances must be compared the millions of people throughout history who have *not* been resurrected. The superior evidence thus lies in favour of scepticism; the balance of probability must tip against the likelihood that Jesus was truly resurrected:

> A wise man proportions his belief to the evidence. In such conclusions as are founded on infallible experience, he expects the event with the last degree of assurance, and regards his past experience as full proof of the future existence of that event. In other cases he proceeds with more caution . . . he considers which side is supported by the greatest number of experiments . . . and when at last he fixes his judgment, the evidence exceeds not what we properly call probability.

- Step 2 The claim that an event has taken place in history must be assessed scientifically. It must be tested empirically and be subject to the normal procedures of historical verification. Reliance on mere hearsay is unacceptable:

> A hundred instances or experiments on one side, and fifty on another, afford a doubtful expectation of any event; though a hundred uniform experiments, with only one that is contradictory, reasonably beget a pretty strong degree of assurance. In all cases, we must balance the opposite experiments . . . and deduct the smaller number from the greater, in order to know the exact force of the superior evidence.

- Step 3 Since the resurrection of Jesus can neither be verified by historical means nor corroborated by similar occurrences, the best we can do is to remain agnostic about whether it happened or not:

> When anyone tells me that he saw a dead man restored to life, I immediately consider with myself

> whether it be more probable that this person should either deceive or be deceived, or that the fact which he relates should really have happened. I weigh one miracle against the other . . . and always reject the greater miracle.

- Step 4 The evidence for Jesus' resurrection is highly unreliable, coming as it does from biased sources and received initially by uncritical believers. Our own experience and that of history shows that people's capacity for believing nonsense is virtually infinite and, therefore, the mere fact that many of the first Christians believed Jesus to have risen from the dead is by itself no indication that he did.

> With what greediness are the miraculous accounts of travellers received . . . But if the spirit of religion join itself to the love of wonder, there is an end of common sense . . . A religionist may be an enthusiast and imagine he sees what has no reality: He may know his narrative to be false and yet persevere in it, with the best intentions in the world, for the sake of promoting so holy a cause.

Conclusion

On all these grounds, therefore, Hume dismisses Christian belief in miracles, especially the resurrection, as unwarrantable. Although he wrote some two hundred years ago, Hume effectively anticipated modern objections. The Christian Church has never really grappled with these but has relied instead on a combination of anti-intellectualism and moral intimidation. These do not make its claims true, though, whatever popes and archbishops might say. The logical agnosticism of Hume is infinitely preferable to the irrational dogmatism of religionists any day.

8
There is an Alternative

They say miracles are past.
William Shakespeare

Miracles do not happen.
Matthew Arnold

In the last chapter we saw our 'hard-edged' agnostic reject Christian claims about Jesus on three grounds: that they could not be proved historically; that the Gospels were no more than the reflections of the writers' own culture and ideology; and that miracles are inherently improbable, if not downright impossible. In this chapter we shall focus on the problem of miracles once more to advance an alternative version of agnosticism – one which remains doubtful about the claims traditionally made about Christ but which, nonetheless, finds a place for miracle stories.

The starting point for this 'soft' agnosticism is the recognition that the rejectionist views put forward in Chapter 7 are themselves vulnerable to exactly the kind of critique 'hard' agnosticism makes against Christianity. That is to say, if Christian beliefs can be debunked on the grounds that they are merely reflections of the culture that produced them, so can the sceptical views of the debunkers. For what is the critique presented in the last chapter if not a summary of objections generated by a so-called 'scientific' world-view? According to this, miracles are simply impossible; therefore any miraculous claim must automatically be rejected. Alternative explanations must be found which fit with a rational understanding of the world. Any phenomenon that does not must be regarded as a fabrication. QED.

But such an argument is as circular and culture-bound as the one it seeks to displace. Both religion and 'hard' agnosticism are, in reality, statements of faith – in one case, faith in a supernatural divinity; in the other, faith in a mechanistic universe governed by iron laws of nature. Either way, we are presented with views which do no more than reflect the culture from which they arose. If we are to be thoroughgoing sceptics about religion – as the 'hard' agnostic urges – we must by the same token be equally sceptical about the dogmatism of our agnostic friend.

In a similar vein, we must take issue with his characterization of history as a collection of totally objective historical facts. The gospels were obviously written with a purpose in mind – to portray Jesus as the Son of God. But, in fairness, *all* history is written with a purpose. There is no such thing as purely factual history. Historical analysis by its very nature is laden with interpretation. To a greater or lesser degree, all history is a matter of selection and evaluation. There are no such things as wholly objective facts. To suppose otherwise is to be naive about how historical method works.

This point is critical. Neither the Gospels in general nor the miracle stories in particular can be dismissed merely because they have been shaped so as to support the case the writers want to advance. Historians on all sorts of subjects do the same.

This does not mean, of course, that we should be incredulous. There are limits to what can be historically acceptable; otherwise we should have to find room for any weird and wonderful claim that came along. This is why 'soft' agnosticism should be regarded as preferable both to its 'hard' relative and to dogmatic religion. A world-view which is both rational and open enough to look for truth behind religious statements without necessarily accepting them at face value is surely more viable than either of its alternatives.

So what would this mean in relation to miracles? How can the clash between dogmatic religion and dogmatic agnosticism be avoided? The answer lies in seeing the New Testament miracle stories not as records of events that actually took place but as devices to convey underlying theological beliefs. They are not to be thought of as literal but as symbolic or parabolic.

Take, for example, the feeding of the five thousand. Traditionally, Christians have used this as an example of Jesus' miraculous powers, thus proving him to be divine. In response to such a view, sceptics came to insist that the miracle could not have happened – loaves and fishes simply do not multiply out of thin air. Either the story was concocted (it never happened) or something took place which was in principle explicable by natural means but which came to be embellished for propaganda purposes (it happened but not in the way the Bible says).

Immediately we see how by setting up the issue in this way, we are forced to choose between two views which are mutually exclusive. We must either accept the story as it appears and has been interpreted down the ages, or we must reject it entirely. But this is a false antithesis. There is a middle way, provided we are willing to renounce both dogmatic extremes. This consists in viewing the feeding story as a myth. That is to say, it should be seen as a story which was *never intended* by the original writers to recount the incident as if it were an historical occurrence. Rather, the story as we find it in the Gospels was designed to tell us something crucial about God, Jesus and ourselves. It is for these underlying insights that we must search.

What might they be? There are various possibilities

which, it must be emphasized, do not rest upon the historical veracity of the story. They remain meaningful whether or not the feeding ever took place. For those prepared to accept a religious interpretation, the passage teaches that:

- Jesus was a man especially holy and able to call upon God in a unique way;
- He was uniquely compassionate;
- In his compassion for others he modelled the way we should behave: we should be generous towards others in need and never confine ourselves to selfish possession of what we have;
- We hold our possessions – even the basic things of life – on trust for the good of others as well as ourselves;
- Ultimately, all we have is from God. He supplies all our needs. We must humbly acknowledge our ultimate dependence on him; and
- Through faith in Jesus Christ, we can discover the generosity of God.

But the beauty of the mythical approach is that it does not require us even to assent to a religious interpretation. It is still possible to find valuable insights even if the religious aspects are disregarded:

- The young boy who offered his food presents us with an example to be followed;
- To act morally means to act out of regard for the needs of others. We cannot be moral and selfish at the same time;
- Human needs can be met by human actions;
- The world contains enough resources for all people. The problem lies not in supply but in distribution and a willingness to share.

These are just some of the possible lessons to be learned from this 'miracle'. Note that none of them depends upon the incident having happened. It is the story *as a story* that conveys beliefs about God, Jesus and ourselves. These beliefs remain even when the miraculous interpretation is stripped away. By using the mythical approach carefully, we can draw lessons from religious stories even when the purely religious aspect is put to one side.

We do not, therefore, have to be forced into choosing between one set of dogmatic beliefs or another. The traditional religious and 'hard-edged' agnostic interpretations are not the only choices. It is possible to view this miracle story – and by extension others too – as containing something valuable, even if we are not convinced about its theology. This is genuine agnosticism: constructive rather than dismissive, open rather than closed.

Application: the Resurrection

If the 'soft' agnostic approach is valid, then we should be able to apply it to the greatest miracle claim of them all – the resurrection of Jesus Christ. How might this work?

First we need to be clear about what we are saying. The mythical method does not depend upon the traditional claim that the dead body of Jesus came back to life three days after his crucifixion. However, it does presuppose that he died. This point is important, for earlier sceptical approaches sought to argue that Jesus never really died while on the cross and that the resurrection was not a return to life after all.

The nineteenth-century German writer, H. E. G. Paulus, is a good example. He claimed that although wounded by the centurion's spear while on the cross, Jesus was not dead when taken down; he was merely in a coma. Consequently, his body was entombed still alive. In the coolness of the cave, Jesus revived and escaped after an earthquake had removed the rock which sealed the tomb. He found some gardener's clothes nearby and went to meet Mary. Being gullible (as were all the disciples), she thought him risen from death and so the story of resurrection spread. Unfortunately, he did not recover from his wounds and after forty days, Jesus said farewell to his followers and disappeared to die.

Such was the kind of attempt by rationalist sceptics of an earlier generation to explain away the resurrection miracle claim. But such a convoluted effort is simply not necessary once we take a mythical approach. For beyond the basic fact that Jesus was crucified (which all but the hardened sceptic accept) we do not need to speculate. The mythical approach carries weight irrespective of the traditional view.

How is this so? We can see in the resurrection story a number of meanings which are important for us whether or not we believe the religious ones.

Religious Meanings

- Death is not the end. Human existence is not terminated by the cessation of mortal life.
- God is active to make this possibility a reality for every human being.
- Jesus Christ, as representative of humanity, has pointed the way to life beyond death through faith in the heavenly Father.
- God is a God of life, not death. The overriding principle which is at work within creation is not decay and destruction but renewal and re-creation.
- Hope of life beyond death presents us with hope in the here-and-now. It thus motivates us to live an ethical life.
- 'Eat, drink and be merry for tomorrow we die' can never be the philosophy of Christians. Its cynical hedonism is based upon a rejection of God's love and life.

However, we are not required to accept any of these in order to find the resurrection story useful. Even stripped of its religious garb, it contains important insights about the human condition:

Non-Religious Meanings

- The tragic death of a good man need not be the end. His beliefs can continue to influence others after his death.
- Even the bleakest of human situations contains within it the seeds of hope.
- We should never give up hope even in the face of death.
- The starkness of death defines the value of life. When we face up to its inevitability we can find a renewal of our lives.
- Given the reality of death, every moment counts. What we do with our lives should be governed by a sense of urgency and purpose.
- Our death can count for something. We can bring hope to others following our death.

Conclusion

In these ways, even the greatest miracle story of them all can yield 'truths' for religionist and non-religionist alike. Treated as a myth or parable, rather than a piece of historical fact, the resurrection of Jesus (which at first sight appears meaningful only for committed Christians) can be seen to contain a wealth of insight even for the agnostic. We are not forced, therefore, to choose between blind, unthinking acceptance of miracles or equally dogmatic rejection of them. For the 'soft' agnostic who is prepared to follow a third way, miracle stories can become rich resources for human living. The challenge presented by an open, constructive agnosticism is by far the most creative option.

9

Truer than You Might Think

I am the resurrection and the life.
Jesus Christ

We keep coming back to two basic issues which determine how we think of Jesus Christ: the reliability of the accounts of his life and death, and the difficulty of believing in miracles – not least the miracle of the resurrection. Indeed, it would probably not be far from the mark to say that of all the problems which surround the person of Jesus Christ, these are the most fundamental.

In this chapter, I shall attempt to supply some answers to these problems. In a few thousand words, of course, I can do no more than sketch the basic arguments. But I hope that even this will be enough to enable the reader to see that there *are* credible replies to both 'hard' and 'soft' agnosticism. As with previous chapters, a list of useful books which go more deeply into the issues will be found at the end of the book.

1. Can the Gospels Be Trusted?

Since the four Gospels are the primary source for our knowledge about Jesus, it is important to know whether we can trust them or not. In practice, this resolves into three issues:

- Can we rely on documents produced so long after the events they describe?

- Was it not inevitable that the Gospel writers would be biased? and
- Why is there no external evidence to support what they say?

1. *Can We Rely on Documents Produced so long after the Events They Describe?*

The first Gospel (probably Mark) was written between thirty and forty years after Jesus' death. This may seem a long gap to us, familiar as we are with technology for producing instant records of events. But in ancient times, it was a remarkably *short* period. The two most important sources for the history of the Roman Empire, for example, are the historians Tacitus and Suetonius. Both wrote at the beginning of the second century AD as did Pliny the Younger, a writer of lesser importance. Yet they recorded events which had taken place not simply thirty or forty years before but in some cases, more than a century. Two instances will illustrate the point.

The first concerns an event about which there is no doubt – the great fire of Rome in 64 AD. This was the fire during which the Emperor Nero allegedly fiddled. We learn about it from both Suetonius and Tacitus. But Suetonius wasn't even born when it happened and Tacitus was only nine (even supposing he witnessed it). Both wrote some decades afterwards; in Tacitus' case, fifty-one years afterwards. Yet their accounts are accepted with considerably less doubt than the Gospel writers' accounts of Jesus written after no less a gap, and in Mark's case a much smaller gap.

The second example makes the point even more sharply. In 49 BC, Julius Caesar crossed the River Rubicon as he returned from Gaul to Italy. The event had a historic significance which resounds even to this day. For in crossing the Rubicon, Caesar committed himself to civil war; thus irrevocably altering the course of Roman history.

Indeed, so decisive was the event that even now we use the phrase 'crossing the Rubicon' to describe actions from which there is no turning back.

It may come as a surprise, therefore, to find that the evidence for Caesar's supposed historic action is incomparably weaker than that supplied by the Gospels for any incident in the life of Jesus. As with the Gospels, we have four accounts of Caesar's action – all of them written by later historians. But the earliest that any of these was born was the mid-first century *after* Christ. In other words, the earliest account was penned about two hundred years after the event. The thirty or forty years' distance between the crucifixion and the arrival of Mark's Gospel seems somewhat small by comparison.

Yet there is more. All four Roman historians relied on a single eyewitness source, that of Asinius Pollio, which has completely vanished. In addition, not only do the accounts vary but Suetonius even alleges in all seriousness that the decisive factor in Caesar's decision was 'an apparition of superhuman size and beauty... sitting on the river bank playing a reed pipe.'

Despite all this, the story of Caesar's crossing is accepted as fact. In contrast, the Gospels – with far greater evidence and testimony to support them – are thought of as mythical. And while the supernatural is apparently no obstacle to trusting the four Romans, it becomes an insuperable obstacle when it comes to the Gospel writers. As the New Testament scholar, Craig Blomberg, has commented, 'Clearly a double standard is at work here.'

So much for comparison between other ancient historical documents and the Gospels. From just these two instances we can see that the Gospels have every right to be taken seriously as historical accounts. What is more, when we ask how Jewish (and surrounding) cultures actually went about the task of recording events, we discover a further reason for allaying our scepticism.

In brief, while modern culture is used to preserving information instantly through film, audio records and on paper, ancient cultures did the opposite. They were essentially *oral* or *storytelling* cultures. This is why the gap between the death of Jesus and the production of the Gospels is not nearly so problematic as we might think. People were trained to remember events and pass them on with accuracy. In Jewish society this was particularly well developed since all three major social institutions – home, synagogue and elementary school – were committed to reinforcing this oral method of retaining and conveying information. As Philo, a Jewish historian of Jesus' time noted, 'all men guard their own customs, but this is especially true of the Jewish nation. Holding that the laws are oracles vouchsafed from God and having been trained in this doctrine from their earliest years, they carry the likeness of the commandments enshrined in their souls.'

As we shall see shortly, this did not mean that they were committed to photographic recall. The exact words uttered by a speaker were not crucial in the ancient world. But the sense, or gist, was. Given the Jewish culture of remembering, we have strong reasons to believe that the Gospel writers convey the fundamentals of any event or speech. As Professor James Dunn has put it:

> We should not assume that the events of Jesus' ministry and his teaching necessarily faded or became confused in the minds of the disciples who had first followed him. In societies where the *spoken* word was the chief means of communication, and where a large portion of education consisted in rote-learning, memories were better trained and almost certainly a good deal more retentive.

The problem of the gap between the crucifixion and the writing of the Gospels, then, is much more a problem of our misunderstanding of the nature of ancient cultures than a problem of accurate recording. The obstacle originates with us, not them.

2. Was It Not Inevitable that the Gospel Writers Would Be Biased?

Matthew, Mark, Luke and John did not write in a vacuum. They worked within a tradition of history writing which reported responsibly. As Luke comments in the opening chapter of his Gospel:

> Inasmuch as many have undertaken to compile a narrative of the things fulfilled among us, just as they were delivered to us by those who from the beginning were eyewitnesses and ministers of the word, it seemed good to me also, having followed all things carefully from the beginning, to write it out for you in an orderly manner, most excellent Theophilus, so that you might know the truth concerning the things of which you were instructed. (Luke 1.1–4)

This tradition operated within a culture of history writing common to ancient societies. When it came to recording events, writers regularly grouped material not just according to chronological sequence but also according to themes and types of events. This explains why variations exist between the Gospels in their placing of events or speeches. One Gospel writer may be concerned, for example, to collect stories about, say, miracles together in one place while another may observe the strict chronological sequence of events as they occurred in Jesus' ministry. The important point to grasp is that this was perfectly acceptable within the conventions of the day. To have variations between documents recording the same events was not a sign of historical inaccuracy but rather an indication that they were genuinely creative in ways that were not only accepted but expected.

Likewise, when recording speeches or sermons, ancient writers felt free to report not the precise words but the thrust of what was said. Thucydides, the Greek historian of the fifth century BC, was honest about this when he declared that 'It was difficult for me to remember the exact substance of the speeches I myself heard and for others to remember those they heard elsewhere and told me of.' Nonetheless, he also acknowledged that he could not simply invent or fabricate what others had said. 'I have given the speeches in the manner in which it seemed to me that each of the speakers would best express what needed to be said about the ever-prevailing situation; but I have kept as close as possible to the total opinion expressed by the actual words.'

The Gospel writers, therefore, wrote according to the historical conventions of the time – which tells us why the words of Jesus are sometimes recorded differently in the Gospels. The writers were not worried whether they had reported the exact speech; they were much more concerned to establish the gist. This was entirely in accordance with contemporary historical method.

Does this rule out the possibility of bias? No, because *all* historical writing is a matter of bias. This is true whether we are speaking of Greek and Roman historians or whether we are referring to modern scholars. It is impossible to write history without some kind of bias. The reason for this is that in order to explain events or develop a narrative, the historian must necessarily select from the welter of information available to her. But how is she to do so unless she already has some kind of working hypothesis in mind? The simple answer is that she cannot. In order to build up a case, she must start with some basic assumptions. Unless she does so, she cannot proceed.

But, of course, once these assumptions are put in place, they continue to guide the process of investigation.

Rather like the police detective who seeks to discover what happened in a crime, the historian attempts to reconstruct events on the basis of a theory as to what *might* have happened. Only as investigation moves forward can the theory be tested. But it cannot move forward without an initial attempt to conjecture what took place.

As historical enquiry into an event proceeds, therefore, the historian is forced to select and evaluate evidence as it comes to light. And again, she is guided by her starting hypothesis. If she is open-minded, she will be ready to modify – or even in extreme circumstances abandon – it if the evidence necessitates. But whatever happens, she has to sift and evaluate. In other words, she must *assess and interpret* as well as record.

Now, if this is the case for modern historians, we should hardly be surprised if the Gospel writers did exactly the same. But this does not mean that they deliberately sought to construct or falsify history simply for their own propaganda purposes.

Why? Because, if they *had* set out to falsify events, we should expect to see counter-gospels written by others seeking to refute what they saw as untruths peddled by Matthew, Mark, Luke and John. To be sure, we do have other so-called 'gospels' which claim to add to what the four say. But (and here is the crucial point) they do not attempt to *refute* them. If the Gospel writers had intended to produce fabrications, they could have made a much better job of it.

Consider, for a moment, the ways in which Jesus is portrayed. If the writers had wanted to concoct a narrative about the Messiah, they would surely have presented Jesus in a radically different light. The Jesus of the Gospels is reluctant to disclose who he is; he refuses expectations for him to lead a political and military crusade against the Romans; he performs miracles but *sotto voce*; and, most significantly of all, he ends up dying in the most humiliating manner possible since crucifixion was the standard means of executing the lowest of low-life criminals.

If the Gospel writers had really been determined to create a Messiah figure, then he would have been politically and militarily committed; he would have asserted himself as a national leader; he would have claimed the mantle of Messiahship as expected and would have used this to promote himself as the people's saviour. He would have sought to sweep to power on a wave of popular nationalism, and even if he had failed in the attempt he would have been portrayed as a hero. If the Gospel writers were intent on propaganda, they were amazingly incompetent.

What is more, they would not have included stories about the resurrection. If Jesus really had been no more than a martyr-cum-sage, the last thing the writers needed to tag on to his life was some weird tale about his coming back from the dead. The inclusion of such a story would only have served to undermine the credibility of their cause. Much better to leave Jesus as a dead martyr than have him appearing in ghost-like fashion for a few weeks to the select few only to have him then disappearing again. Who would believe such nonsense? – unless, of course, it were true.

We will come back to this point shortly. Suffice it to say that if the objective of the Gospel writers had been to produce an official 'life of Jesus' for propaganda purposes, they went about it in an unbelievably ham-fisted way, despite having thirty or forty years to get it right. It seems much more credible to accept that they wrote history in good faith according to the methods and conventions prevalent in their time. And if this was the case, we can't avoid the implications.

3. Why Do We Not Have Evidence from Sources Other than the Gospels?

The short answer is that we do, but it is nothing like as

detailed. We have already seen how it is not unusual for our knowledge of ancient history to depend on only a few sources. By contrast, the Gospels provide a superabundance of historical evidence. The problem is that because they claim so much about their central character, we instinctively feel the need for corroboration.

In fact, there is such corroboration, though on nothing like the scale the Gospels provide. The Gospels remain the only detailed accounts of Jesus of Nazareth we have. What Roman and Jewish historians supply is confirmation that Jesus was a real historical figure, that he was crucified under Pontius Pilate and that a burgeoning movement quickly sprang up which worshipped him as divine.

The most famous of these historians is Josephus, a Jewish writer who wrote in the final decade of the first century. In a renowned passage, he speaks of Jesus thus:

> At this time there appeared Jesus, a wise man, *if indeed one ought to call him a man*. For he was a doer of amazing deeds, a teacher of persons who receive truth with pleasure. He won over many Jews and many of the Greeks. *He was the Messiah*. And when Pilate condemned him to the cross, the leading men among us having accused him, those who loved him from the first did not cease to do so. *For he appeared to them the third day alive again, the divine prophets having spoken these things and a myriad of other marvels concerning him*. And to the present, the tribe of Christians, named after this person, has not disappeared.

This has been a much disputed text among scholars. The words in italics are by general agreement reckoned to have been later inserted into the original by Christians, since it is difficult to believe that a Jewish historian who became an apologist for Rome would have written them; they are simply too blatant a declaration of Christian belief.

But even stripped of the controversial sentences, what

this passage shows is that the basic framework for the arrest, trial and crucifixion of Jesus contained in the Gospels must be reckoned as reliable. Moreover, as Josephus testifies, Christianity was still going strong a generation after its founders had gone. Josephus is close enough to the first years of the Church to have been able to deny its historical basis (which he did not), yet sufficiently detached to distance himself from any attempts at propaganda unsubstantiated by fact.

When we turn to Roman sources, we quickly realize that they had little time for Christianity. Tacitus, writing in AD 115, accused Nero of persecuting Christians as scapegoats to take attention away from himself for the destruction of Rome by fire in AD 64: 'Consequently, to get rid of the report [that he had started the fire] Nero fastened the guilt and inflicted the most exquisite tortures upon a class . . . called Christians by the populace.' Significantly, Tacitus continues, 'Christus, from whom the name had its origin, suffered the extreme penalty during the reign of Tiberius at the hands of one of our procurators, Pontius Pilatus . . . Accordingly, an arrest was made of all who pleaded guilty: then, upon their information, an immense multitude was convicted.'

This extract yields a number of important clues. First, that, by AD 64, Christianity had spread to the centre of the empire. Second, that a large number of believers were willing to die rather than recant. And third, that Tacitus accepted the historical fact of Jesus' death. Once again we find that sources external to the Bible confirm the basic facts about Jesus' death and the surprising upsurge of a movement devoted not to his memory as a martyr but to the belief that somehow he had risen from death.

And so we come to the central claim of the Christian faith: the resurrection of Jesus.

2. Miracles and the Resurrection

In Chapters 7 and 8, we saw how belief in miracles remains a stumbling block for many. On one hand our 'hard' agnostic would have no truck with the biblical stories at all while on the other, our 'soft' agnostic was prepared to concede some place for them provided they did not have to be understood as literal, historical events.

The problem with both these views is that they just do not fit the way biblical writers thought. For them the miracle stories were not fanciful tales, however laden they might be with meaningful insight in the sense the 'soft' agnostic would contend. The Gospel writers believed they were faithfully recording actual events in the life of Jesus Christ.

Both positions, therefore, avoid the central issue: what the biblical writers themselves were seeking to say. Here, the 'soft' agnostic has few grounds for his view that they were deliberately using a 'mythical' approach. For if one thing is abundantly clear, it is that the Gospel writers believed they had collected stories of miraculous events that actually occurred in Jesus' ministry. In fact, the so-called 'mythical' approach turns out to be no more than a later imposition by nineteenth- and twentieth-century sceptics who could not cope with the possibility of miracles.

Chief among their grounds was the belief that miracles are inconsistent with a modern, scientific view of the universe. In a cosmos governed by immutable laws of nature, not only is there no room for miracles, there is no need. The biblical writers simply did not understand this and were consequently deluded.

For both types of agnostic, then, their rejection of miracles is based upon a prior assumption: that miracles do not, and cannot, happen.

We need to recognize this for what it is: a statement of faith every bit as dogmatic as the belief that miracles *do* happen. Once we grasp this, we quickly realize that the rejection of miracles does not follow from a careful consideration of the evidence with an open mind, but from a prior belief that miracles *cannot* take place.

How then can we proceed? I would suggest that a genuinely open position will judge each claim on its merits, neither presupposing in advance that a miracle has taken place nor that it has not. The commitment involved in such an approach consequently becomes not an ideological commitment one way or the other but a genuine search for truth.

But how might we apply this to the Gospels? This brings us back to the resurrection. For if we can accept that Jesus really did rise from the dead, we shall surely be able to accept that other, lesser miracles could have occurred. As Christians have claimed from the beginning, the resurrection of Jesus is *the* foundation for faith.

Jesus' Resurrection Considered

Arguments Against

The case against the resurrection of Jesus runs something like this: resurrections do not happen now, and outside the Bible nobody has ever seen or experienced one. We are therefore wholly reliant upon the say-so of a bunch of writers who were highly motivated to concoct the story of their hero rising from the dead. They wanted to promote the Christian faith, so what better way to do it than to dream up a sensational tale about Jesus coming back to life? Considered dispassionately, we can arrive at a number of alternative explanations which fit with scientific laws and do not require supernatural intervention. In short, the resurrection can be explained without recourse to miraculous fairy stories-cum-propaganda.

This kind of argument is superficially plausible but fails

completely when subjected to close scrutiny. It has the air of a pub discussion in which its proponents know just enough to sound convincing but not enough to realize they have failed to think things through. This will become clear as we take the points in turn.

1. Resurrections Do Not Happen

This is really a version of the closed-mind position we noted earlier in relation to miracles. Consequently it shares all the weaknesses we observed in such a view. The statement 'Resurrections do not happen' is not a factual claim but is a disguised ideological claim about the nature of the universe. In effect, it says, 'Resurrections can *never* happen because if they did, they would breach my scientific view of how the world works.' The fundamental problem with this view, of course, is that it is so blinkered that it reduces every phenomenon to a single type of explanation – the so-called 'scientific' one. But even that is highly questionable for all the reasons we saw in Chapters 2 and 3. The biblical scholar, A. M. Hunter, makes a valid point when he comments that 'Gone are the days when scientists could dogmatically declare that miracles, because they were "violations of the laws of nature" were therefore impossible.'

John Polkinghorne is one such scientist. Formerly Professor of Mathematical Physics at Cambridge and President of Queen's College, he is now a Christian priest. Having thought deeply about miracles in general and the resurrection in particular, he concludes both that miracles are possible and that the resurrection of Jesus is credible. Two passages from his writings make the point clearly. In his book, *Quarks, Chaos and Christianity*, Polkinghorne argues that:

> The question of miracle is not primarily scientific, but *theological.* Science simply tells us that these events are

> against normal expectation. We knew this at the start. Science cannot exclude the possibility that, on particular occasions, God does particular, unprecedented things. After all, he is the ordainer of the laws of nature, not someone who is subject to them. (pp. 82–3)

Elsewhere he contends that:

> We know that the world is full of surprises, so that confidence that we know beforehand what is reasonable and possible is strictly limited. Unprecedented or previously unexplored realms of experience may very well prove contrary in character to the familiar and the everyday. One has only to utter the words 'quantum theory' to make the point. (*Serious Talk*, p. 91)

2. The Motivation of the Gospel Writers Was Suspect

In addition to the difficulties we have already seen with this view, it also falls into the trap of assuming that commitment to a belief automatically renders a person's testimony invalid. But why should this be so? While it is true that in some cases people will perjure themselves for a cause, we should not assume in advance that this will always be the case.

Imagine David, for example. He is a Jew who survived the Holocaust. He can recount stories of absolute horror from his time in the death camps of Hitler's Germany. He is a committed anti-Nazi. Does this make his recollections untrue? Does it invalidate his testimony?

Or take Bernadette. She is a Rwandan refugee forced out of her home by the genocide of 1994. She has seen her husband and three sons butchered by people whom they counted as neighbours in their home village. Driven from her country, she has spent two years in a refugee camp in Zaire. In 1996 she returned home, feeling at last able to tell her story. Does the awfulness of her experience invalidate her eyewitness accounts? Does her deep determination to see justice done against the killers of her family mean that we can no longer trust the evidence she has supplied?

Finally, think of Milan. He is a Bosnian young man who was taken from his village by Serbs in 1993 along with all the other men. They were driven to an isolated spot 10 kilometres away and shot. Milan escaped solely because he was wounded but remained alert enough to feign death. When the bodies were piled on top of him, he was just able to survive until nightfall and crawl away. In the morning, the corpses were shovelled into a mass grave and buried. From that day to this he has carried an abiding hatred of Serbs; but does that mean that the events never happened or that he will automatically lie about them?

Clearly the answer in all three cases must be 'no'. Neither David nor Bernadette nor Milan can be held to be a liar simply because of the depths of their experiences. The mere fact that they had suffered terribly would not discount their testimony in a court of law.

By the same token, we should not discount the testimonies of the Gospel writers and their sources. Just because they had a message to proclaim does not mean that they would fabricate the story of the resurrection. Logically speaking, it is equally likely that they had a message to proclaim because the resurrection actually took place. And for reasons we shall shortly come to, the possibility of fabrication is highly unlikely indeed.

3. *Alternative Explanations for the Resurrection*

Once we rule out the possibility that Jesus was truly resurrected, we are left with three other possibilities: (i) Jesus didn't die on the cross – he lost consciousness and was later revived; (ii) the so-called 'resurrection appearances' were nothing more than hallucinations; and (iii) the disciples stole the body.

Explanation (i) we considered earlier to be inherently

implausible because it just does not fit the evidence. Number (ii) has greater plausibility but must also be rejected. Why? Because (a) the appearances of the resurrected Jesus were too many and too varied realistically to have been hallucinations. He did not appear only to the twelve disciples but to lots of individuals and on one occasion to a crowd of five hundred. (b) Why should the Gospel writers have deduced merely from hallucinations that Jesus had risen from the dead? They could just have easily supposed the appearances to be those of a ghost. In fact, this would have been much more plausible to their contemporaries since belief in individual resurrection was both uncommon and outlandish. If they truly had wanted to convince as many people as possible, they would have been much better off avoiding the notion of resurrection altogether. To claim that a man had come back to life was the easiest route to becoming laughing stocks – unless, of course it were true. (c) The effect of these 'hallucinations' was nothing short of revolutionary. Which is more plausible? – to believe that mere psychological illusions caused the explosive birth of the Christian faith or that the resurrection itself did?

As for (iii), we have to ask why the disciples would have wished to steal the body in the first place and what they did with it. Given the weirdness of the claim that Jesus had been resurrected, they would have had little motivation to do so. Moreover, they would have spent the rest of their lives living and (in some cases) being tortured for what they knew to be a lie. It simply does not add up. In the words of Professor James Dunn, 'There must have been something about these first encounters . . . which pushed them [the first Christians] to what was an extraordinary conclusion in the context of that time. A careful jury would have to ask why the first Christians drew such an unusual conclusion.'

So much, then, for alternative explanations. None of

them is inherently more plausible or sustainable from the evidence than the conclusion that the Gospel writers proclaimed the resurrection because it took place.

The argument, however, needs to go further. Having discussed the case against the resurrection, we must now turn to the positive case in favour.

Arguments For

1. The High Estimate of Jesus soon after His Death

It is striking that within a matter of years after his death, Jesus of Nazareth was being spoken of not as a great man but as God. Now it was not uncommon for individuals to be idolized or deified. But it was only non-Jews who did so. The Romans, for example, were ready to impart deity to their leaders at the drop of a toga. The truly amazing thing is that it was *Jews* who first proclaimed the divinity of Christ. So strong was their commitment to belief in only one God – Yahweh – that they were often thought of as atheists because they refused to accept other alleged divinities. And so, when it was from the mouths of devout Jews that the name of Jesus first came to be uttered as divine and furthermore worshipped, we have to ask why. To quote Professor Dunn once more, 'For a *Jew* to speak of a *man*, Jesus, in terms which showed him sharing in the deity of *God*, was a quite astonishing feature of early Christianity.'

Yet this is what happened. The first disciples, good Jews though they were, within weeks of the crucifixion were telling all and sundry that the man from Nazareth executed as a common criminal was, in fact, God! And within a further short space of time, another Jewish leader, Saul of Tarsus, had reneged on his fierce opposition to this new sect and had joined them to become one of their most powerful advocates.

While these facts do not amount to a knock-down case,

they do suggest that something astounding happened soon after the death of Jesus. His followers, and those who in turn joined them, were sure about what that was – the resurrection. If we are to account for the Jesus phenomenon we must supply a persuasive alternative.

2. The Transformation of the Disciples

Two weeks before Jesus was arrested, the disciples were squabbling and boasting about which of them should occupy positions of power in the new Messianic kingdom they thought he would soon establish. Within less than a fortnight, they were in hiding, ready to disown him once he had been taken into custody. On the day of his execution, none of them showed up (except perhaps for the young man John).

This was the state of Jesus' male followers immediately after his death. How, then, do we explain their complete transformation within a matter of days? From being a bunch of demoralized, terrified cowards they turned into a band of determined, unafraid proclaimers of the faith, boldly preaching the message that Christ was alive and active in their midst. The hallucination hypothesis seems totally unable to bear the weight of this change. Similarly, the accusation that they stole the body collapses. For who would have set about the task of converting the world with such fervour and commitment on the basis of a confidence trick? What is more, it is inconceivable that these selfsame men would have endured persecution, torture and death knowing that it had all begun with a lie. Con artists are not known for their self-sacrifice.

Likewise, it is hard to believe that the faith would have spread so rapidly and to such effect (remember Tacitus' comments about the influence of Christianity in Rome?) had its instigators deliberately been lying. At some point, the Jewish authorities would have produced the corpse of Jesus and put an end to this new religious brushfire. That they *did* not suggests that they *could* not; the body was risen.

3. The Witness of the Church

From its earliest days, the Christian Church pinned itself to the incredible claim that its founder, having died in public view, had returned to life as a demonstration of his divinity. This belief – weird as we have seen – remained the rock on which successive generations of Christians built their lives to the present day. It gave impetus to the missionary zeal of the New Testament, it gave backbone to the believers who were tortured or killed in the years of persecution which began within months of Jesus' death, and it sustains millions throughout the world today.

Moreover, from the first generation onwards, Christians have claimed not simply to believe intellectually that Christ rose from the dead; but that in some mysterious way, they experience his living presence here and now. Once more, it is hard to equate all this with either a living lie or a self-deception. Both possibilities, of course, remain open. But the inquirer must ask herself which is more credible, given the cumulative balance of evidence: that the resurrection was a hoax-cum-illusion or that it happened?

4. The Significance of Women

At first sight, this might seem an odd piece of evidence to wheel out. However, it is highly significant that the Gospel writers clearly insist that the first witnesses to the resurrection of Jesus were women. A brief reading of their accounts of the first Easter day shows that it was the women who met the risen Christ first of all and who then carried the news back to the incredulous men. There is no doubt that the writers wished to make it clear that women were the primary witnesses to the Easter events.

This is nothing short of astonishing. If Matthew, Mark, Luke and John really had rigged their accounts, the last thing they would have done was to put the women at the centre. The reason? Simply that the contemporary status of women was so low that no one would have believed them. Women's testimonies, for example, were inadmissible as evidence in a court of law because women were regarded as unreliable witnesses merely because they were women. Even in our own times, this remains the case in some Middle Eastern societies. To have made the truthfulness of the resurrection stories dependent upon the word of women, therefore, would have been suicidal on the part of the Gospel writers – unless, of course, they really did witness what they said.

5. The Absence of Tomb Veneration

There is a well-known Sherlock Holmes tale entitled *The Hound of the Baskervilles*. In it, the great detective concludes that the crime must have been committed by someone known to the family who murdered his victim overnight while the household slept. When questioned, he comments that if there had been an intruder, the dog would have barked. It didn't. Therefore, the hound must have known the perpetrator.

A similar kind of logic applies to the absence of any evidence that the early Christians venerated, or paid homage to, the supposed tomb of Jesus. If there had been a body still buried at the site, we can be sure that believers would have gathered there regularly to venerate it and to worship. Such was the common custom of the day which persists even to the present. The tombs of Abraham and David continue to be venerated at Hebron and Jerusalem respectively, as is the tomb of a near contemporary of Jesus, the charismatic rabbi Honi, 'the circle-drawer'.

But there remains no evidence that the tomb of Jesus was venerated at any time during the first three centuries after his death. The conclusion? In the words of James Dunn:

This strange silence, exceptional in view of the religious practice of the time, has only one obvious explanation. The first Christians did not regard the place where Jesus had been laid as having any special significance because no grave was thought to contain Jesus' earthly remains. The tomb was not venerated, it did not become a place of pilgrimage, because the tomb was empty!

Summary

The arguments I have set out here will not convince the hardened sceptic. For those prepared to be open-minded, however, and to consider the case even-handedly, the outcome may be rather different. True, there is no single argument that will wipe out all doubt. But the cumulative weight of evidence, I would suggest, points much more towards the likelihood that Jesus really was raised from death than any of the alternatives. If this is the case, the agnostic must begin to ask some searching questions as to how long his agnosticism can hold up.

Conclusion

10
Decisions

You must make your choice. Either this man was, and is, the Son of God; or else a madman or something worse.

C. S. Lewis

So where do we go from here? I have attempted to show how three of the most common obstacles to Christian belief need not be obstacles at all. Rather, when carefully considered with a genuinely open mind, they can lead to a fresh awareness of the Christian faith as a set of beliefs that it is possible to hold with intellectual integrity. This is a long way from the easy dismissal of Christianity with which we began.

But where does that leave agnosticism? The simple answer is: faced with a massive problem. For if the arguments of preceding chapters have carried any force at all, the reader by now will have realized that agnosticism cannot long survive as a bolt-hole from making up our minds about the evidence for Christian belief.

In particular, the agnostic has to make up his mind about the person of Jesus Christ. The commonest response when faced with this question is to say something like, 'Well, of course, he was a good man and a courageous moral teacher. But as for all that stuff about being the Son of God – I'm not so sure . . .'

The problem with this view is that it can be no more than a temporary halting place. For the more we read the accounts of Jesus' life and the reports of his sayings, the harder it becomes to remain equivocal. Why? Simply because the character, claims and teachings of Jesus force us to a decision: what shall we do with this man who claimed to be God?

Three decisions confront us if we are serious about the person of Jesus Christ. First, we need to decide whether he was who he said he was – whether we are prepared to accept his words about himself. Second, we must decide why he died – was it just a tragedy or was there more to it than that? And third, we must decide what our response ought to be. In these final pages, we shall look at each of these in turn, not with a view to sustaining an agnostic stance but to committing ourselves one way or the other. Make-your-mind-up time has arrived.

1. Who Was Jesus?

The Gospels are absolutely clear as to who Jesus was – the Son of God. Time after time, the writers affirm that he was not simply another holy man with a hot line to the Almighty but that he was God-made-flesh. Now, of course, it would be easy to dismiss this as impossible, as pre-scientific mumbo-jumbo. But once we embark on *that* road we are back into the dogmatic so-called 'scientific' world-view that rules out miracles as a matter of prior assumption. And for the reasons we noted in the last chapter, this will not stand up.

So we are left with a massive claim about which we have to make up our minds: was Jesus who he said he was? We might attempt to water down the enormity of such a claim by concentrating on his moral teaching. But this falls at the first hurdle. For the words of Jesus are all of a piece or they are nothing. The same Jesus who gave the moral precepts so widely accepted as inspiring is the one who declared himself to be the Son of God, equal with God and having come from God. He claimed to forgive sins, heal the sick, raise the dead – all because God had given him the authority to do so. If such a man stepped into our midst today, we should think him either conceited beyond belief or just plain mad. Yet we think neither of these things about Jesus. In the words of C. S. Lewis, 'A man who was merely a man and said the sort of things Jesus said would not be a great moral teacher. He would either be a lunatic – on the level with a man who says he is a poached egg – or else he would be the Devil of Hell.'

Here, then, is the dilemma: do we accept all that Jesus said, or none of it? We can't pick and choose on the grounds that some bits make us uncomfortable or don't happen to fit with our world-view. We must either accept it all or reject it all. To quote C. S. Lewis again, 'Let us not come with any patronising nonsense about His being a great human teacher. He has not left that open to us. He did not intend to.'

But this merely leads to a second dilemma: what do we do with the Gospels? We have seen how difficult it is to regard them as unhistorical fictions made up by Christian propagandists. If that was their authors' intention, they are incredibly poor products. The Jesus of the Gospels is simply not the figure of whom propaganda is made. If the accounts of his life were intended to be that, the writers were unbelievably incompetent. And if that was the best they could manage, it is astonishing the Christian movement sprang up at all.

Yet it did spring up – around the belief that the man from Nazareth had risen from the dead and that his death and resurrection were somehow tied together in the purposes of God. It was not his moral teaching that provided the impetus for the birth of Christianity. Rather, it was around the contention – witnessed to by many hundreds of people – that he had risen from the dead and had appeared to his followers that the movement began to grow. And so we arrive at a third dilemma: what to do with the resurrection? Given the argument of the last chapter, simply doing nothing is not an option. We have to accept the resurrection or reject it. That is the stark choice it puts before us.

2. Why Did Jesus Die?

It is impossible to be agnostic about the death of Jesus Christ for one simple reason: either it meant nothing or it meant everything. If the first, then countless millions throughout history have been labouring under a delusion. If the second, then we cannot remain neutral about it. Once again we find ourselves faced with a decision that refuses to go away.

What are the possibilities? If Jesus was no more than a sage-cum-martyr, then the most we can say is that his death inspired others in a way that no other death has. We have already seen how as early as thirty years or so after the crucifixion, 'large numbers' (Tacitus' phrase) were prepared to be tortured and killed rather than recant their Christian faith. The brutal fact is that if Jesus' death and the preaching of his followers was merely a self-delusion, the first Christians were – and millions since have been – living a lie. Even worse, those who had begun the lie must have known what they were doing and where it would lead. In other words, they must have been prepared to see lives wasted for a cause they knew to be a deceit.

Yet is this credible? From what we know of the first disciples, they were nothing like this. Immediately before and after Jesus' death they were terrified. To imagine that within the space of a few weeks they had turned into courageous preachers risking their lives for the gospel one minute, only to become cold-hearted cynics the next, willing to sacrifice their fellow believers for what they knew to be a lie, is simply not believable. The evidence just does not fit.

We must look elsewhere, then, for explanations of Jesus' death. At one level, of course, it was the result of a political act. The Jewish leaders did not want him around any longer and the Roman governor, Pontius Pilate, saw no point in resisting them. At a more profound level, though, the crucifixion meant much more. And as the first Christians came to see, its significance was far greater than anyone had realized.

We can summarize the meaning of Christ's death in three words: *suffering, alienation and hope*. Taken together, they encompass its purpose and result. All Christian teaching about the crucifixion is embraced by them. In the space that remains we shall glimpse something of their force.

At its most obvious, the crucifixion was an act of unimaginable agony. To be nailed to a wooden cross for hours amounted to nothing less than torture. Yet Christians have insisted from the beginning that in and through the suffering of his Son, God was doing something unique for the human race. What was it?

The key to understanding why the *suffering* of Jesus was so important lies in a simple but crucial idea: that in his death Jesus was somehow taking upon himself the suffering of the world. This notion is not susceptible to scientific analysis. It is one of those ideas – like self-sacrificial love – which either makes sense or not. The reason why Christians have held it to be both sense-making and true is that it offers a way of understanding the crucifixion which addresses the most fundamental human reality of all – that we are born into a world of suffering and pain which seems to fly in the face of any notions of divine goodness, love or justice.

But Jesus the God–man hanging on the cross enables us to live in such a world and strive for its betterment without despair. As the Son of God, he experiences the ultimate degradation and suffering, and so identifies himself and his heavenly Father with the lot of the human race. On the cross, God suffers as we suffer. He demonstrates his solidarity with us. There is no more poignant way of experiencing what it means to be human.

Viewed from this perspective, the death of Jesus begins to make sense. For how else could God identify with humanity unless he were to go through the realities of human existence to the end – through suffering to death itself? Christ's death thus ceases to be meaningless and starts to reveal the depths of God's love for his creatures. As St John put it in the third chapter of his Gospel: 'God so loved the world that he gave his only Son' (John 3.16).

But it does not stop there. The crucified Christ does not simply suffer with us. The cross deals with a further fundamental human reality – that of *alienation*. 'Alienated from whom (or what)?' is the obvious next question. The answer is: alienation from God, from the world and from one another. St Augustine put it succinctly when he stated that in each of us there is a God-shaped hole which only God can fill. Why? Because he made us for himself and until we find our fulfilment and purposefulness in him, we shall simply thrash around for substitutes, be they materialism, sex, politics, revolution, good causes or whatever. Whether we like it or not, human beings are a profoundly alienated race.

But how does the death of Jesus relate to this? Here we need to go back to the notion of Jesus' solidarity with humanity. Almost his last words on the cross were: 'My God, my God why have you forsaken me?' Theologians have puzzled for millennia over the precise meaning of that cry of dereliction (as it is known). Theories abound. But for the moment the point we need to hold fast to is that just as Jesus mysteriously caught up our suffering into his own, so he took upon himself our alienation. Our separation from God, from others, from life itself, he experienced for himself in his death and dying. He was the representative human being, facing in our place the horrors of 'separatedness' from truth, love, life. Can we even begin to grasp it?

Which brings us to *hope*. Jesus bearing our suffering and alienation is of a piece with this central theme of the Christian faith. A Christ who suffered as we do and who stands in our place is a tremendous thought. But the power of Jesus' death goes even further. As the title of a famous Puritan book put it, in the death of Christ we have the death of death itself. This does not mean, of course, that those who believe in him will never have to go through the process of mortal death. This is manifestly not the case. Rather, in going through human death and rising again, Jesus offered us hope for new life beyond the grave.

In this way we see how the crucifixion and resurrection are tied together. Jesus suffers pain, death and alienation as we do. But that is not the end. He conquers death; he defeats it; he destroys its power. He brings hope.

But, as we might expect, it is not quite as simple as that. There is the question of inbuilt human sinfulness – the innate tendency to prefer self above God, above others, above everything. Only in exceptional moments do we seem able to transcend this. The sad fact is that most of the time we are self-centred, choosing what suits *us* and ignoring God and our fellows. This, we find, brings us back to alienation – to be understood this time not merely as a sense of lostness but as a self-determined desire to have our own way as we quest for autonomy.

Jesus is blunt about the self-centred human condition we all share. It cuts us off from God, enthrones self and demotes others. We find ourselves trapped by it, unable to break free or even realize we *need* to. Left to ourselves we would spend our lives seeking ever-increasing self-fulfilment until it killed us (quite literally).

But it does not have to be that way. The death of Christ makes a difference. We can experience freedom from this false quest through faith in the crucified and risen One. Such a choice will not be easy (and certainly not cheap since the cost was borne by Christ himself). We shall find that the new life of which Jesus spoke has its obstacles and problems. Those evangelists who promise health, wealth and happiness if only we will accept their gospel are promising something that Jesus refused to offer.

What he does hold out, however, is something infinitely more valuable: the promise of relationship with God. This is no trivial matter. It deserves our serious consideration. The question is: what will be our response?

3. What Shall I Do about This Man?

In my experience, the greatest obstacle to Christian belief is not intellectual or moral. It is fear. Fear of committing oneself to something which might change one's life. And that is exactly what faith in Jesus Christ will do. It will not leave us alone to continue as if nothing had happened. It will grab us and turn our lives upside down. It will transform us from searching for meaning, truth and purpose into people who have found these. It will give us new life, new horizons, new challenges. But most of all, it will give us relationship with the One who made us, who died for us and who rose for us. And in doing so it will liberate us to love Christ, ourselves and others.

This is the choice that faces each of us and which demands a response. We can equivocate no longer. Agnosticism must give way either to atheism or to faith. The bolt-hole is shut: the decision awaits.

Further Reading

The possibilities for further reading on all three topics are almost endless. I have selected books under each heading for their readability combined with a high level of accessible argument. In the case of Part One, all are written by practising scientists.

Part One: Science and Faith

C. J. S. Clarke, *Reality Through the Looking Glass: Science and Awareness in the Postmodern World*. Floris Books 1996.
Paul Davies, *God and the New Physics*. Penguin 1983.
Paul Davies, *The Mind of God*. Penguin 1992.
Rodney Holder, *Nothing But Atoms and Molecules?* Monarch 1993.
John Polkinghorne, *Quarks, Chaos and Christianity*. Triangle 1994.
John Polkinghorne, *Serious Talk*. SCM 1995.
David Wilkinson and Rob Frost, *Thinking Clearly About God And Science*. Monarch 1996.

Part Two: The Problem of Suffering

David Cook, *Thinking About Faith*, chapter 5. Inter-Varsity Press 1986.
Peter Cotterell, *Is God Helpless?* Triangle 1996.
C. S. Lewis, *The Problem of Pain*. Fount 1977.
Peter Vardy, *The Puzzle of Evil*. Fount 1992.

Part Three: Jesus Christ

James D. G. Dunn, *The Evidence for Jesus*. SCM 1985.
Alister McGrath, *Jesus: Who He Is and Why He Matters*. Inter-Varsity Press 1987, 1994.
Michael J. Wilkins and J. P. Moreland, *Jesus Under Fire*. Paternoster Press 1996.
N. T. Wright, *Who Was Jesus?* SPCK 1992.

List of Sources

Chapter 1: The Triumph of Science

Matthew Arnold, 'Dover Beach', reprinted in *The Oxford Library of English Poetry*, vol. III (Book Club Associates 1993), p. 166.
Peter Atkins, *The Creation*, quoted in Mary Midgley, *Science as Salvation* (Routledge 1992), p. 89.
Peter Atkins, *The Creation*, quoted in Bryan Appleyard, *Understanding the Present* (Picador 1992), p. 151.
Ian Barbour, *Issues in Science and Religion* (SCM Press 1968), p.26.
J. D. Bernal, *The Social Function of Science*, quoted in Midgley, *Science as Salvation*, p. 5.
Charles Darwin, *Autobiography*, quoted in Midgley, *Science as Salvation*, p. 102.
Richard Dawkins, *The Blind Watchmaker* (Penguin Books 1988), p. 26.
Sigmund Freud, *The Future of an Illusion* quoted in Appleyard, *Understanding the Present*, p. 75.
Sigmund Freud, quoted in Francis Bridger and David Atkinson, *Counselling in Context* (HarperCollins 1994), p. 107.
Galileo, quoted in Colin A. Russell, *Cross-Currents* (Inter-Varsity Press 1985), p. 45.
Stephen Hawking, *A Brief History of Time* (Bantam Press 1988), p. 13.
Kit Mouat, *What Humanism Is about* (Barrie and Rockliff 1963), p. 143.
Nehru, quoted in Appleyard, *Understanding the Present*, p. 1.
William Tyndale, quoted in Keith Thomas, *Religion and the Decline of Magic* (Penguin Books 1973), p. 29.
C. H. Waddington, *The Scientific Attitude*, quoted in Midgley, *Science as Salvation*, p. 6.
C. H. Waddington, quoted in Ian Barbour (ed.), *Science and Religion* (SCM Press 1968), p. 58.

John Wheeler, *Quantum Theory and Measurement*, quoted in Midgley, *Science as Salvation*, p. 208.

Chapter 2: The Chastening of Science

Paul Feyerabend, *Against Method*, p. 11, quoted in C. J. S. Clarke, *Reality Through the Looking-Glass* (Floris Books 1996), p. 32.
Mary Midgley, *Science as Salvation* (Routledge 1992), p. 52.
Jacques Monod, *Chance and Necessity*, quoted in Rodney D. Holder, *Nothing but Atoms and Molecules?* (Monarch 1993), p. 137.
Harold Wilson, quoted in Ben Pimlott, *Harold Wilson* (HarperCollins 1993), p. 304.

Chapter 3: Science and Faith Revisited

Bacon, quoted in Rodney D. Holder, *Nothing but Atoms and Molecules?* (Monarch 1993), p. 60.
Niels Bohr, quoted in Paul Davies, *God and the New Physics* (Penguin Books 1984), p. 100.
Robert Boyle, quoted in Colin A. Russell, *Cross-Currents* (Inter-Varsity Press 1985), p. 62.
Paul Davies, *God and the New Physics* (Penguin Books 1984).
Paul Davies, *The Mind of God* (Penguin Books 1993), p. 231.
Paul Davies and J. R. Brown, *The Ghost in the Atom* (Cambridge University Press 1990), p. 84.
Paul Davies and John Gribbin, *The Matter Myth* (Penguin Books 1992), p. 3.
David Deutsch, interviewed in Davies and Brown, *The Ghost in the Atom*, p. 84.
Bryce de Witt, quoted in Paul Davies, *Other Worlds* (Penguin Books 1990), pp. 136–7.
Einstein, quoted in Davies, *God and the New Physics*, frontispiece.
Jacques Monod, *Chance and Necessity*, quoted in Holder, *Nothing but Atoms and Molecules?*, p. 137.
John Polkinghorne, *Serious Talk* (SCM Press 1995), p. 17.
Karl Popper, quoted in Holder, *Nothing but Atoms and Molecules?*, p. 45.
A. N. Whitehead, *Science and the Modern World*, quoted in Russell, *Cross-Currents*, p. 67.
Ludwig Wittgenstein, *Tracatus Logico-Philosphicus*, quoted in Bryan Appleyard, *Understanding the Present* (Picador 1992), p. 16.

Chapter 4: God, Suffering and Scepticism

Thomas Alitzer, *Radical Theology*, quoted in Eliezer Berkovits, *Faith after the Holocaust* (KTAV Publishing House 1973), p. 63.

Darrell Fasching, *Narrative Theology after Auschwitz* (Fortress Press 1992), p. 21.

Anton Gill, *Journey back from Hell* (Grafton Books 1988), pp. 26–7.

Irving Greenberg, quoted in Fasching, *Narrative Theology after Auschwitz*, p. 15.

Adolf Hitler, *Mein Kampf*, quoted in Fasching, *Narrative Theology after Auschwitz*, p. 20.

Thomas Hobbes, *Leviathan*, quoted in *The Concise Oxford Dictionary of Quotations* (World Books 1971), p. 105.

Martin Luther, *On the Jews and their Lies*, quoted in Fasching, *Narrative Theology after Auschwitz*, p. 20.

Richard Rubenstein, *After Auschwitz*, quoted in Dan Cohn-Sherbok, *Holocaust Theology* (Lamp Press 1989), p. 82.

Chapter 5: Other Voices: Some Alternative Agnosticisms

Eliezer Berkovits, *Faith after the Holocaust* (KTAV Publishing House 1973), p. 7.

Fritjof Capra, *The Turning Point* (Flamingo 1983), p. 410.

Benjamin Creme, *The Reappearance of the Christ and the Master of Wisdom*, quoted in Walter Martin, *The New Age Cult* (Bethany House Publishers 1989), p. 21.

Richard Dawkins, *The Blind Watchmaker* (Penguin Books 1988), p. 169.

Mary Baker Eddy, *Science and Health with Key to the Scriptures*, quoted in John Hick, *Evil and the God of Love* (Fontana 1968), p. 30.

Adolf Hitler, quoted in Alan Bullock, *Hitler and Stalin* (Fontana Press 1993), p. 150.

Shirley Maclaine. See also her comment that 'Maybe the tragedy of the human race was that we had forgotten we were each Divine', *Out on a Limb* (Bantam Books 1983), p. 347.

John Stuart Mill, *Three Essays on Religion*, quoted in Hick, *Evil and the God of Love*, p. 34.

William Paley, *Natural Theology*, quoted in Dawkins, *The Blind Watchmaker*, p. 5.

Jane Roberts, quoted in Martin, *The New Age Cult*, p. 25.

Joyce Watson, *A Guide to the New Age for Confused Christians* (Grove Pastoral Series 47, Grove Books 1991), p. 5.

Chapter 6: God in the Wasteland

Richard Bauckham, *Moltmann: A Messianic Theology in the Making* (Marshall Pickering 1987), p. 87.
Eliezer Berkovits, *Faith after the Holocaust* (KTAV Publishing House 1973), p. 71.
Albert Camus, quoted in Stephen Travis, *I Believe in the Second Coming of Jesus* (Hodder and Stoughton 1988), p. 46.
Heinrich Himmler, quoted in Berkovits, *Faith after the Holocaust*, p. 72.
Jürgen Moltmann, *The Crucified God* (SCM Press 1974), p. 22.
Moltmann, *The Crucified God*, p. 46.
John Polkinghorne, *Serious Talk* (SCM Press 1995), p. 52.
Bertrand Russell, quoted in Travis, *I Believe in the Second Coming of Jesus*, p. 16.
The Long Silence, quoted in Stephen Gaukroger, *It Makes Sense* (Scripture Union 1989), pp. 26–7.

Chapter 7: Man, Myth or God?

Henry Ford, quoted in the *Concise Oxford Dictionary of Quotations* (World Books 1971), p. 87.
David Hume, *An Inquiry Concerning Human Understanding*, Section X, quoted in Ernst and Marie-Luise Keller, *Miracles in Dispute* (SCM Press 1969), pp. 52–3, 62.
Albert Schweitzer, quoted in John Bowden, *Jesus: The Unanswered Questions* (SCM Press 1988), p. 35.

Chapter 8: There is an Alternative

Matthew Arnold, *Literature and Dogma*, quoted in the *Concise Oxford Dictionary of Quotations* (World Books 1971), p. 12.
William Shakespeare, *All's Well that Ends Well*, act 2, scene 3.

Chapter 9: Truer than You Might Think

Luke 1.1–4 (RSV).
John 11.25 (RSV).
Craig Blomberg, 'Where do we start studying Jesus?' in Michael J. Wilkins and J. P. Moreland, *Jesus under Fire* (Paternoster Press 1995), p. 37.
James Dunn, *The Evidence for Jesus* (SCM Press 1985), pp. 2, 73, 61–2, 67–8.

A. M. Hunter, *Jesus: Lord and Saviour* (Eerdmans 1976), p. 63.
Philo, *The Embassy to Gaius*, quoted in Darrell L. Bock, 'The words of Jesus in the Gospels: Live, Jive, or Memorex?' in Wilkins and Moreland, *Jesus under Fire*, p. 80.
Pliny the Younger, see Edwin M. Yamauchi, 'Jesus outside the New Testament: What is the evidence?', in Wilkins and Moreland, *Jesus under Fire*, pp. 215–17.
John Polkinghorne, *Quarks, Chaos and Christianity* (Triangle 1994), pp. 81–2.
John Polkinghorne, *Serious Talk* (SCM Press 1995), p. 91.
Tacitus, see Yamauchi, 'Jesus outside the New Testament: What is the evidence?', in Wilkins and Moreland, *Jesus under Fire*, pp. 215–17.
Suetonius, see Yamauchi, 'Jesus outside the New Testament: What is the evidence?', in Wilkins and Moreland, *Jesus under Fire*, pp. 215–17.
Thucydides, *History of the Peloponnesian War*, quoted in Bock, in Wilkins and Moreland, *Jesus under Fire*, p. 79.

Chapter 10: Decisions

C. S. Lewis, *Mere Christianity* (Fount 1997), p. 52.
Tacitus, *Annals 15.44*, quoted in Edwin M. Yamauchi, 'Jesus outside the New Testament: What is the evidence?', in Michael J. Wilkins and J. P. Moreland, *Jesus under Fire* (Paternoster Press 1995), p. 216.